D0953812

THE NEW ILLUSTRATED GUIDE TO
MODERN
WARSHIPS

THE NEW ILLUSTRATED GUIDE TO

MODERN
WARSHIPS

TONY GIBBONS & DAVID MILLER

A Salamander Book

©Salamander Books Ltd. 1992
129-137 York Way,
London N7 9LG,
United Kingdom.

ISBN 0-8317-5053-7

This edition published in 1992 by
SMITHMARK Publishers, Inc., 112
Madison Avenue, New York, NY 10016.

SMITHMARK Books are available for
bulk purchase for sales promotion and
premium use. For details write or
telephone the Manager of Special
Sales, SMITHMARK Publishers, Inc.,
112 Madison Avenue, New York, NY
10016. (212) 532-6660.

All rights reserved. Except for use in a
review, no part of this book may be
reproduced, stored in a retrieval system
or transmitted in any form or by any
means, electronic, mechanical,
photocopying, recording or otherwise,
without the prior permission of the
publisher.

All correspondence concerning the
content of this volume should be
addressed to Salamander Books Ltd.

This book may not be sold outside the
United States of America or Canada.

Contents

Ships are arranged alphabetically within national groups.

Credits

Authors: Tony Gibbons was for many years an art director in advertising before becoming a full-time freelance author and illustrator specializing in subjects of a maritime nature.

David Miller is an ex-officer in the British Army who now writes as a full-time author on subjects of a military and technical nature.

Editor: Bob Munro

Designers: John Heritage and Lloyd Martin

Line drawings: ©Siegfried Breyer and ©A.D. Baker (US warships, courtesy *Jane's Fighting Ships*)

Picture research: Tony Moore

Filmset by The Old Mill

Color reproduction by Scantrans Pte.

Printed in Hong Kong

Photographs: The publisher wishes to thank all the official international governmental archives, weapons systems, manufacturers and private collections who supplied photographs for this book.

Santa Cruz (TR-1700) Class

Patrol submarines
Two boats (S 41-S 42); two building (S 43-S 44); two projected (S??-S??).

Country of origin: Argentina.
Displacement: 2,116 tons surfaced (2,264 tons submerged).
Dimensions: Length overall 216.5ft (66m); beam 23.9ft (7.3m); depth 21.3ft (6.5m).
Armament: Six 21in (533mm) tubes for 22 AEG SST 4 wire-guided torpedoes.
Propulsion: Four diesels, one electric motor (8,000shp); one shaft; 15kts surfaced (25kts submerged).

In the mid-1970s a programme of submarine construction was planned which would incorporate a European yard. Contracts were signed in November 1977 with West Germany's Thyssen Nordseewerke for the first two submarines, which were to be built at Emden, with four more boats to be built in Argentina using parts and management skills from the German company, at Astilleros Domecq Garcia of Buenos Aires. The first boat, *Santa Cruz* (S 41), was laid down in December 1980, launched in September 1982 and commissioned in October 1984. The second vessel, *San Juan* (S 42), was commissioned in November 1985. Two more units were laid down in Argentina, *Sante Fe* (S 43) in October 1983 and *Santiago Del Estero* (S 44) in August 1985, but completion of these now depends upon the acquisition of foreign sales and no further work is being carried out until a foreign buyer is found. A fifth and sixth vessel have not been laid down. Initially funds were guaranteed by West Germany, but in 1986 they gave permission for the two Argentinian boats to be sold.

The basic design can be enlarged to take a small nuclear reactor, but although the naval staff favour this there is now little political will as this would entail collaboration with Brazil after the 1988 defence production agreement with that country. The vessels are capable of carrying ground mines as well as a good array of torpedoes, including 22 AEG wire-guided torpedoes with active/passive homing to 15nm (28.5km) at 23kts, plus swim-out discharge US Mk 37 torpedoes.

Below: An unusual view of the first-of-class, *Santa Cruz* (S 41), during construction in the yard of Thyssen Nordseewerke. *San Juan* (S 42), the second-of-class, was also built and launched here.

Automatic reloads take only 50 seconds and the Signaal Sinbads onboard fire control system can handle three torpedoes simultaneously.

Range is 12,000nm (22.800km) at 8kts surfaced, drastically reducing to 20nm (38km) at 25kts. Submerged at 6kts, range is 460nm (874km). Speed on the surface is 15kts, and 25kts dived.

Maximum endurance is 70 days. Diving depth is 270m (890ft), and Krupp Atlas CSU 3/4 search and attack and Tomson Sintra DUUX5 sonars are fitted.

Basically, these are successful designs only needing a crew of 26, but financial restaints in Argentina have delayed their development. An enlarged version with a nuclear reactor and improved range now seems a long way off due to the unhealthy economic climate.

Below: With her name and "place of birth" displayed on the sail, *Santa Cruz* (S 41) undergoes her first set of sea trials in the North Sea. Note the low mounting of the forward hydroplanes.

Tupi (209 Type 1400) Class

Patrol submarines
One boat (S 30); two building (S 31-S 32); one projected (S 33).

Country of origin: Brazil.
Displacement: 1,260 tons surfaced (1,440 tons submerged).
Dimensions: Length overall 200.1ft (61m); beam 20.3ft (6.2m); depth 18ft (5.5m).
Armament: Eight 21in (533mm) tubes for 16 Marconi Mk24 Tigerfish Mod 1 torpedoes.
Propulsion: Four diesel electric, one electric motor (5,000hp); one shaft; 11kts surfaced (21.5kts submerged).

To secure the defence of NATO's northern flank it was decided to obtain a small but effective submarine fleet for Norway. By the end of the 1950s the existing choice of vessels were obsolete and new boats were needed. The United States was prepared to bear half the cost of such a programme, and a suitable design was being developed at that time in the Federal Republic of Germany.

Although small, it had good operational and offensive qualities so an agreement was drawn up between Norway and West Germany for 15 boats to be built in Germany. This eventually became the 207 Class.

All 15 boats were quickly built by Rheinstahl Nordseewerke, of Emden, using the pre-prepared sectional structure system whereby individual sections of the hull were built separately, thus greatly reducing construction time; in some cases down to just over four months.

Following the delivery and successful trials of this batch, Denmark decided to obtain two boats of this type (to be built in their own yard), but difficulties with revised specifications caused problems and they were not completed until 1970. Meantime, mid-1967 was the start of a lean period for the German U-boat

industry as plans for an improved type were postponed. Strenuous efforts were now made to obtain orders, but the small 205 type was no longer needed and it seemed profitable to offer a larger version that could act as a fleet submarine to Latin American navies eager to acquire modern submarines, as their existing WW2 fleet submarines became obsolete. As considerable design and construction capacity existed a revised plan was worked out in 1967 with increased dimensions, much larger battery capacity giving improved underwater performance, and a stronger propulsion unit. Endurance was an estimated 50 days.

Displacement was to be under 1,000 tons and the short length of about 179ft (54m) enabled the boat to be successfully used on inshore missions. Good submerged qualities were given top priority. The boat had a smooth hull and, coupled with the enlarged submerged propulsion unit, a maximum speed of 22kts was achieved, which was the fastest speed attained by a standard boat up until that time. This type became known as the 209. The units built for Brazil are of a latter type with an increased surface displacement of 1,260 tons. Machinery is four diesel electric MTU 12V-493-A280 GA and one Seimens electric motor driving a single screw. Surface speed is 11kts with 8,200nm (15,580km) range at 8kts and 400nm (760km) at 4kts submerged.

Fire control is provided by Ferranti Kafs-AIO action data automation and Sperry Mk 29 inertial navigation. Sonars are Krupp Atlas CSU-83/I, hull-mounted passive/active search and attack. The first boat, *Tupi* (S 30), was laid down at Howaldtswere-Deutsche Werf (Kiel) in March 1985, launched in April 1987 and commissioned in December 1988. The second and third units *Tamboiq* (S 31) and *Timbira* (S 32), were built by Arsenal De Marinha, Rio De Janeiro and are due to enter service in 1992/93. The fourth unit, *Tapajos* (S 33), has not been started. Original plans called for six units, but because of delays in construction this seems unlikely to be achieved.

Below: Built at Kiel, Germany, *Tupi* (S 30) was launched on 28 April 1987 and commissioned into service with the Brazilian Navy on 20 December 1988. The boat carries a 30-man crew.

Halifax Class

Helicopter-carrying frigates
One ship (FFH 330); 11 building (FFH 331-FFH 341).

Country of origin: Canada.
Displacement: 4,750 tons full load.
Dimensions: Length overall 444.6ft (135.5m); beam 53.8ft (16.4m); draught 16.1ft (4.9m).
Aircraft: One Sikorsky CH-124A Sea King ASW helicopter.
Armament: Eight Harpoon SSM launchers; two eight-cell VLS launchers for Sea Sparrow SAMs; one 2.25in (57mm) Bofors SAK Mk2 DP gun; one 0.8in (20mm) Mk 15 gatling CIWS; six 12.7in (324mm) Mk 32 ASW torpedo tubes.
Propulsion: CODOG. Two General Electric LM-2500-30 gas turbines (47,494shp); one SEMT-Pielstick 20PA6-V280-BTC diesel (11,780bhp); two shafts; 29.2kts.

Following the completion of four classes of frigate and one class of destroyers between 1951 and 1973, Canadian naval planning underwent a long period of stagnation and no further surface warships were constructed for many years. This situation was exacerbated by the abortive plans to procure no less than 12 nuclear-propelled attack submarines (SSNs): a vast programme which absorbed most of the money, resources and attention of the Royal Canadian Navy (RCN) for some years.

By the mid-1970s the RCN was faced with block obsolescence of its frigate force in the late-1980s and two steps were taken. One was the updating of the Tribal (DDH-280) class destroyers (see page 12-13) and the other the ordering

of a new design of ASW frigate — the Halifax (or "City") class. This new programme was announced in December 1977, orders being placed for six vessels at a time. The first batch, ordered in July 1983, are being completed between 1990 and 1992, while the second batch was ordered in December 1987 for commissioning between 1993 and 1997. A possible third batch is still under consideration, but may be replaced by an order for diesel-electric submarines. The first-of-class, HMCS *Halifax*, was launched on 19 May 1988 and started her trials on 6 August 1990.

The Halifax class ships displace 4,750 tons, large by "frigate" standards, and are designed to accommodate a sizeable ASW helicopter, namely the CH-124A Sea King or, in the future, the Agusta-Westland EH.101 Merlin. Main armament comprises eight Harpoon SSMs, mounted abaft the stack, although, in order to save money, the fire-control system for these missiles will not be of the latest version. Air defence is provided by Sea Sparrow SAMs using eight vertical launch tubes sited amidships, between the mast and the stack: in war an additional twelve reloads will be carried. The gun is a 2.25in (57mm) Bofors, which although appearing small in calibre for a warship this size, is claimed by the makers to be more effective than any 3in (76mm) gun currently on the market (a comment clearly aimed at the OTO Melara Compact, which is virtually the *only* 3in (76mm) gun in production!). A US Navy developed Mk 15 0.8in (20mm) CIWS is installed, situated aft on the hangar roof.

Considerable effort has been devoted to incorporating "stealth" features to defeat hostile radar and sonar detection systems. There was a plan to lengthen the hull of vessels in the second and third batches, to increase the number of Sea Sparrows carried and to improve accommodation, but this has been shelved.

Below: The first-of-class, HMCS *Halifax* (FFH 330), seen during its initial sea trials. The programme has experienced several delays, but the potential of the basic design is undoubted.

Tribal (DDH 280) Class

Destroyers
Four ships (DDH 280 — DDH 283).

Country of origin: Canada.
Displacement: 5,100 tons full load.
Dimensions: Length overall 423ft (128.9m); beam 50ft (15.2m); draught 14.5ft (4.4m).
Aircraft: Two Sikorsky CH-124A Sea King ASW helicopters.
Armament: Mk 41 VLS for 32 Standard SM2 SAMs; one OTO Melara 3in (76mm) DP gun; one Mk 15 0.8in (20mm) gatling CIWS; two triple Mk 32 torpedo tubes.
Propulsion: COGOG. Two GE LM-2500-30 gas turbines (47,494shp); two GM Allison 570KF gas turbines (12,788shp); two shafts; 30kts.

For many years the Royal Canadian Navy (RCN) relied on British designs for its destroyers and frigates, which were built in Canadian yards. In 1951, however, they decided to build their own designs and the result has been a series of unusual looking ships, packed with innovations and ideally suited to their role in the inhospitable waters of the North Atlantic.

First came a series of 19 frigates, completed between 1956 and 1964. The St Laurent class (six ships) was followed by the Restigouche (three ships) and the Improved Restigouche (four ships) classes. The design was further developed into the Mackenzie class (four ships) and, finally, the Annapolis class (two ships), which is armed with two 3in (76.2mm) guns, six 12.7in (324mm) ASW torpedo tubes and one Sea King helicopter. Only the latter two classes remain in service, with the Annapolis class due to be the last to strike in 1996.

The Tribal (DDH 280) class destroyers first appeared in 1972-73. Like their predecessors they had a distinctive appearance, but this is undergoing major changes as a consequence of the 1987-1993 Tribal Update and Modernization Program (TRUMP) refits. (The specification data given above are for the post-TRUMP modified ships.) The RCN has always used larger helicopters in relation to ship size than other navies and the Tribals carry two Sea Kings. Landing is assisted by the "Beartrap", a cable which is attached to the hovering helicopter and which then hauls the aircraft onto the deck.

The new Halifax class ships (12 are on order) will join the fleet from 1992 onwards. Although designated frigates, they are actually larger than the Tribal class destroyers.

Below: A pre-TRUMP view of HMCS *Huron* (DDH 281), the second Halifax class destroyer acquired by the RCN. Note the highly distinctive angle of the funnel and the prominent 5in (127mm) foredeck gun.

Hainan (Type 037) Class

Fast attack craft — patrol
100 craft (approx.): **People's Republic of China** — 60 + ; **Bangladesh** — eight; **Egypt** — eight; **North Korea** — six; **Pakistan** — four.

Country of origin: People's Republic of China.
Displacement: 400 tons.
Dimensions: Length 192.9ft (58.8m); beam 23.6ft (7.2m); draught 7.2ft (2.2m).
Armament: Four Chinese 2.25in (57mm) AA guns; four Soviet 1in (25mm) cannon; four RBU 1200 ASW RL; two depth-charge projectors; mines.
Propulsion: Four diesels (8,800bhp); four shafts; 30kts.

The Soviet Union built some 150 SO1 class large patrol boats in the late 1950s and 1960s, some of which went to the People's Republic of China (PRC). Following the split between the two countries the Chinese Navy started producing its own designs, which, for ease of production, were based closely on Soviet craft already in service. One of these was the SO1, which was lengthened and modified in minor ways to produce the Hainan class. Production started in 1964 and has continued at a slow but steady rate until today, with new craft replacing the older boats of the class.

There are two twin 2.25in (57mm) mounts — one forward, one aft — and two twin 1in (25mm) mounts. Depth-charge racks and two RBU 1200 are mounted, but ASW capability is restricted. Two French sonars were obtained for trials in the late-1980s in an effort to overcome this deficiency.

Above: A flotilla of
Hainan class fast
patrol craft off the
Chinese coast. Of 400
tons full load dis-
placement, these
craft are designed in
the PRC and are still
being built, albeit
at a modest rate. The
weapon illustrated
above is a four-
barrel MBU-1800
ASW rocket launcher.

Left: Hainan class
patrol craft on a
firing exercise. All
recent visitors to
the PRC attest the
very high standards
maintained by the
PLA-Navy: the ships
and men are always
extremely smart and
the ships are in
excellent condition.
It is of interest
that throughout the
upheavals of the
1960s the PLA-Navy
retained traditional
sailors' uniforms.

Luda Class

Guided-missile destroyers
16 ships (DDG 105-DDG 110, DDG 131-DDG 134, DDG 161- DDG 165); two
building.

Country of origin: People's Republic of China.
Displacement: 3,960 tons full load.
Dimensions: Length overall 433ft (132.0m); beam 42ft (12.8m); draught
13.1ft (4.0m).
Armament: Six HY-2 SSM launchers; four 5.1in (130mm) DP guns; eight
2.25in (57mm) or 1.45 (37mm) AA guns; four 1in (25mm) AA cannon; two
12-tube ASW rocket launchers; four BMB-2 depth charge mortars; two
depth charge racks; mines.
Propulsion: Two sets geared turbines (60,000shp); two shafts; 32kts.

The Chinese Navy is one of the most powerful in the Far East. After the People's Republic of China (PRC) was established in 1949 initial equipment was a mixture of Japanese, American and British designs captured from the Nationalists. The Soviet Union supplied a number of elderly vessels to augment this motley

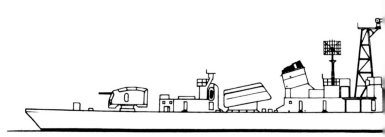

**Above: The Luda class vessels were the first major warships to be
designed and built in PRC shipyards. They are based on the Soviet
Kotlin class, but with an enhanced armament fit.**

force, including four Gordi class destroyers (two of which remain in service) and four Riga class frigates, all of which are still in service. Submarines and patrol boats were also supplied. Following the political breach with the Soviet Union in 1956, China continued to build a number of warships to Soviet designs.

Modified versions of Soviet designs were then produced. Five Jiangnan class frigates (modified Riga class) were completed between 1964 and 1968, followed by the largest of the current Chinese surface warships, the Ludas, which first appeared in 1972. Sixteen were built, but one was lost due to an explosion in 1983. These have similarities with the Soviet Kotlin class, but are larger, with a different stern, bigger superstructure and different armament. The main weapon is the Hai Ying-2 SSM, six being mounted in two triple launchers, one between the stacks and the other abaft the after stack.

Secondary armament varies between ships, some having eight 2.25in (57mm) AA guns, others 1.45in (37mm) guns. Equipment and sensors alsos vary. At one stage it was proposed to install US CIWS and ASW torpedoes, but this fell through with the 1989 weapons embargo. One ship has a helicopter deck and hangar aft, resulting in the loss of one triple SSM launcher, a gun turret and four ASW mortars. Improved sensors have also been fitted. The names of two ships are not known, but the remaining 14 in the class are: *Jinan, Xian Yinchuan, Xining, Kaifeng, Dalian, Nanjing, Hefei, Chongging, Zunyi, Changsha, Nanning, Nanchang,* and *Guilin.*

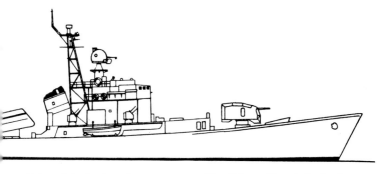

Below: A Luda class destroyer at sea. The Chinese Navy is by far the most numerous in the Far East, but its ships still lack the standard of equipment sported by the West's major navies.

Shanghai Class

Fast attack craft — patrol
500 craft (approx.). **People's Republic of China** — 330 approx.; many in foreign navies.

Country of origin: People's Republic of China.
Displacement: 135 tons.
Dimensions: Length 127.3ft (38.8m); beam 17.7ft (5.4m); draught 5.6ft (1.7m).
Armament: Four Chinese 1.45in (37mm) AA guns; four Soviet 1in (25mm) cannon; two RBU-1200 ASW RL (on some boats); two depth-charge projectors; mines.
Propulsion: Two M50F-4 diesels (2,400shp); two 12D6 diesels (1,820shp); four shafts; 28 5kts.

The Chinese Navy now possesses the largest force of light craft in the world, operating Chinese versions of a number of Soviet designs, including Osa and Komar guided missile patrol boats and P6 class torpedo boats. It also operates a number of Chinese-designed boats, including the Huchuan class hydrofoils. Over a third of its light craft, however, are a number of different versions of the Shanghai class patrol boat. These are conventional general-purpose craft, with certain similarities to the Soviet SO1 class.

Above: The simple lines of a Shanghai Type II fast attack craft.

The Shanghais are mainly intended for coastal work and have a relatively powerful armament of light weapons, which normally includes four twin automatic cannon mounts: two of 1.45in (37mm) calibre and two of 1in (25mm). Not surprisingly, in a boat built in such large numbers over such a long period, there are many minor differences between production series in armament, radars and bridge structures, and technically there are five versions of the class.

Many have been exported to Asian, Middle Eastern and African navies. Licence-production is being undertaken in Romania, which operates some 25 of the type, and eight were supplied by the PRC to Albania.

Below: With over 300 in service with the PLA Navy, and another 100 or so in foreign service, the Shanhgai class patrol craft is one of the PRC's great maritime success stories.

19

XIA Class

Nuclear-powered missile submarine
One boat (406).

Country of origin: People's Republic of China.
Displacement: 8,000 tons submerged.
Dimensions: Length overall 393.6ft (120m); beam 33ft (10m); depth 26.2ft (8m).
Armament: Six 21in (533mm) tubes for 12 CSS-N-3 SLBM.
Propulsion: One nuclear reactor; turbo electric drive; 22kts submerged.

When the first unit, *Xia* entered service in 1987, China finally joined the nuclear "club". First laid down at Huludao Shipyard in 1987 and launched in April 1981, much time was taken up with test-firing the CSS-N-3 two-stage missile, and it was not until September 1988 that a successful launch was carried out. A second vessel was launched in 1982, but work on this has stopped and plans to build improved groups have been shelved. For China to maintain a credible nuclear submarine force, at least three vessels are needed. The present missiles have a range of about 1,421nm (2,700km) and only targets in the Soviet Far East can be threatened. An improved version known as CSS-NX-4 is under development but may not be ready until the late-1990s.

The hull form resembles the earlier USS *George Washington* and the shape does not guarantee quiet submerged running. Diving depth is 984ft (300m) and speed is 22kts submerged.

Right: Caught as she submerges, this view of *Xia* clearly shows the "turtleback" below which lie up to 12 CSS-N-3 SLBMs.

Below: An ES5G, a Chinese predecessor of the Xia class boat, fires a C-801 SSM during an exhaustive series of trials at sea.

Clemenceau Class

Aircraft carriers
Two ships (R98-R99).

Country of origin: France.
Displacement: 32,700 tons full load.
Dimensions: Length overall 869.4ft (265.0m); width (over flightdeck) 168.0ft (51.2m); draught 28.2ft (8.6m).
Aircraft: Typically, 16 Super Etendard, 10 F-8E(FN) Crusader, 3 Etendard IVP, 7 Alizé, 2 + Alouette III or Dauphin helicopters.
Armament: Two Crotale EDIR SAM systems, four 3.9in (100mm) Model 1953 DP guns.
Propulsion: Two sets Parsons geared-turbines (126,000shp); two shafts; 32kts.

In the early post-war years the French Navy operated five aircraft carriers. The oldest was the pre-war, French-built carrier, *Béarn*, which was of limited value. Two were lent by the USA in 1946, *Bois Belleau* and *La Fayette* being returned in 1960 and 1963 respectively. The third, *Dixmude*, a converted cargo ship, was transferred from the United Kingdom in 1945, but was used mainly as an aircraft transport. The best was the *Arromanches*, formerly HMS *Colossus*, the name ship of her class of "light fleet carriers", which was lent by the Royal Navy in 1946 and purchased outright in 1951; she was eventually scrapped in 1970.

The French Navy replaced these with a class of carriers of French design, *Clemenceau* (R98) and *Foch* (R99), which were laid down in the 1950s, incorporating all the advances in carrier practice made in the early post-war period. They have served the French Navy well, operating in the Pacific in support of the remaining French colonial territories and of the nuclear test programme, as well as supporting operations closer to home; for example, off Lebanon and in the Gulf War.

They are of conventional design, with an 8deg angled deck, a single-deck armoured hangar, a mirror landing-aid designed in France, two lifts and two steam catapults, one forward and one on the angled-deck. The stack is blended in with

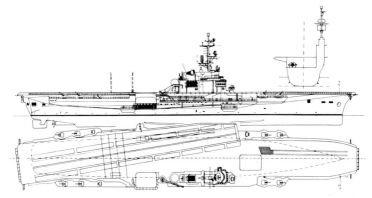

Above: *Clemenceau* (R 98), France's first purpose-built carrier.

Above: A Dassault Etendard IVM strike aircraft takes the wire on the angled deck of *Clemenceau* (R 98) during an exercise.

Below: *Clemenceau* at sea with her air wing complement parked on the flight-deck. Visible from front to rear are Vought F-8E (FN) Crusaders, Dassault Etendards and Breguet Alizés.

the superstructure as on US Navy carriers. *Clemenceau* was fitted with bulges following her working-up trials and similar devices were incorporated into *Foch* during construction.

The French developed a series of aircraft specifically for service on these ships, including Dassault Etendard and Super Etendard strike fighters, and the Breguet Alize ASW aircraft. The selected fighter, however, was the US Navy's·Vought F-8E Crusader, 42 of which were delivered in the late-1960s as the F-8E(FN).

Both ships have received several major refits during their service, the most important of which was that needed to enable them to operate Super Etendard fighters: *Clemenceau* in 1977-78 and *Foch* in 1980-81. Both are now approaching the end of their useful lives and *Clemenceau* demonstrated some well-publicized mechanical problems during her Middle East deployment during the Gulf War. They are due to be paid off in 1988 (*Clemenceau*) and 2002 (*Foch*).

Two new nuclear-powered carriers have been ordered. The first, which is due to be launched in 1992, is to be named *Charles de Gaulle* (R 91) and will replace *Clemenceau*; the second, as yet unnamed, will replace *Foch*. They will be powered by two pressurized-water nuclear reactors, giving them virtually unlimited endurance. These 36,000 ton displacement ships will have an 8.3deg angled deck and will carry 35-40 aircraft, of which the most important will be the Dassault-Breguet Rafale M. The Rafale flight demonstrator for this programme is already flying. It is highly probable that Grumman E 2C Hawkeye aircraft will be purchased for the AEW role, whilst French helicopters will be employed for the ASW mission.

Below: A pair of Etendard IVMs in the foreground sit amongst a gaggle of more capable Dassault Super Etendard strike fighters.

Above: The aviation complement aboard the second-of-class ship, *Foch* (R 99), is limited to helicopters such as these Super Frelons.

D'Estienne D'Orves (Type A 69) Class

Patrol frigates
20 ships: **France** — 17 (F 781-F 797); **Argentina** — three (31-33).

Country of origin: France.
Displacement: 1,330 tons.
Dimensions: Length 262.5ft (80.0m); beam 33.8ft (10.3m); draught 9.8ft (3.0m).
Armament: Four MM38 Exocet SSM launchers; one 3.9in (100mm) Model 1968 DP gun; two 0.8in (20mm) AA cannon; one Creusot-Loire 14.75in (375mm) ASW RL; four fixed torpedo tubes.
Propulsion: Two SEMT-Pielstick 12 PC 2 V400 diesels; two shafts; 23.3kts. (Specifications are for later ships in the class).

The French Navy developed a series of small escort vessels, starting in the 1950s, which led to the Commandant Riviére class. These are diesel-powered ships, with a full load displacement of 2,170 tons and a speed of 25kts. Built between 1957 and 1965, their original main armament was three single 3.9in (100mm) guns, but one of these has since been replaced by four Exocet SSM launchers. They can also carry two landing-craft and an 80-man commando for operations in French colonial territories. Six remain in service, together with one modified ship built to test a CODAG powerplant, but they are now being stricken, with the last due to decommission in 1993/94.

The next class is the D'Estienne d'Orves class, which are slightly smaller and mainly intended for ASW operations in coastal waters, although they are frequently used for operations overseas. The single 3.9in (100mm) gun is mounted forward, immediately ahead of the large bridge. ASW weapons comprise a large 14.75in (375mm) rocket launcher mounted atop the deckhouse aft and four fixed tubes for L-3 or L-5 torpedoes, for which no reloads are carried.

Above: *D'Estienne d'Orves*. Note Exocet launchers beside the funnel.

As built between 1972 and 1984, they carried no missiles, but the five ships in the Mediterranean Squadron now mount two MM38 Exocet launchers; the remainder mount four MM40s. Another modification has been the raising of the stack. As so often happens, more equipment has been squeezed into these ships and while the original ships displaced 1,250 tons, this has increased in the last batch to 1,330 tons. A small commando detachment of an officer and 17 men can be carried.

These handy little frigates have proved economical and reliable in service, but, somewhat surprisingly, have attracted only one export order. Two of a slightly modified design were ordered by the South African Navy in 1976, but this order was cancelled by the French government and the ships were then sold to Argentina in 1978 Subsequently, the Argentine Navy ordered a third. One of these, *Geurrico* (32), was seriously damaged by shore-based Royal Marines during the Argentine invasion of South Georgia in April 1982.

The three oldest ships are due to pay-off in 1996, followed by the remainder at regular intervals, with the last going in 2004. Their replacement is the Floréal class (3,000 tons) of patrol frigates, of which the first was launched in 1990.

Below: Leaving a trail of exhaust smoke in its wake, an MM 38 Exocet SSM roars away from the French Navy's *Premier Maître L'Her* (F 792). Two MM 38 Exocets can be carried by these vessels.

Georges Leygues (F70 ASW) & Cassard (F70 AA) Classes

Guided-missile destroyers
Seven ships (D 640-D 646); two ships (D 614-D 615).

Country of origin: France.
Displacement: 4,350 tons full load.
Dimensions: Length overall 456.0ft (139.0m); beam 45.9ft (14.0m); draught 13.5ft (4.1m).
Aircraft: Two Aerospatiale Lynx ASW helicopters.
Armament: Eight Exocet SSM launchers (four only in first two ships); one Crotale Navale EDIR eight-cell SAM launcher; one 3.9in (100mm) Model 1968 DP gun; two Oerlikon 0.8in (20mm) AA cannon; two catapults for L 5 ASW torpedoes.
Propulsion: CODOG. Two Rolls-Royce Olympus TM3B gas-turbines (52,000shp); two SEMT-Pielstick 16PA6-CV280-BTC diesel engines (10,400bhp); two shafts; 30kts.

These well-designed and capable ships represent a notable achievement on the part of the designers, who have managed to produce one hull which is capable of two different weapon and sensor fits to undertake two roles. Developed from the Tourville (F 67) class, the first of the ASW version was commissioned in 1979. The first four (*Georges Leygues, Dupleix, Montcalm* and *Jean de Vienne*) form the F 70 ASW (1) class and the remaining three (*Primauguet, Le Motte-Picquet* and *Latouche-Treville*) the F 70 ASW (2) class; a proposed eighth ship was cancelled as an economy measure. The main differences between the two

versions are that the later group have a towed sonar array, rather than a variable-depth sonar (VDS), and the bridge has been raised by one deck level to overcome the problems the first group of vessels experienced when operating in bad weather.

After the seven ASW vessels the F 70 AA was designed to provide the anti-aircraft and anti-missile defences for a carrier task group or a merchant convoy. Designated the Cassard class, these ships have completely different weapons, sensor and propulsion systems mounted in an identical hull; four were originally authorized, but two were cancelled for financial reasons. *Cassard* entered service in 1988 and *Jean Bart* in 1991. The main AA armament is the Standard SAM missile system which was formerly installed in the two T 47 class destroyers; these use a twin-arm Mk13 launcher, but may use a VLS launch system in due course. These two ships also have the French SADRAL close-in missile system, with one launcher either side of the hangar, the latter housing a single Aerospatiale Lynx helicopter. As with the F 70 ASW, the F 70 AA mounts a single 3.9in (100mm) gun forward and eight MM 40 Exocet missile launchers amidships.

Propulsion for the F 70 AA is four diesel engines rather than the two gas-turbine, two diesel mix (CODOG) in the F 70 ASW. It is claimed that this is because the latest diesels are almost as light and as easy to maintain as gas-turbines, but do not require such large air intakes and exhaust trunking. This latter point is demonstrated by the curiously shaped stack in which the 3-D radar antenna is mounted atop the combined exhaust ducts and radar mast.

These nine ships provide the French Navy with a strong force of seven ASW and two AA frigates, which will serve well into the 21st Century.

Below: The fourth and final F70 ASW (1) vessel for the French Navy was *Jeanne de Vienne* (D 643). A product of the Brest Naval Dockyard, she was commissioned into service on 26 May 1984.

Le Redoutable & L'Inflexible Classes

Nuclear-powered ballistic missile submarines
Five boats (S 610-S 614); one boat (S 615).

Country of origin: France.
Displacement: Le Redoutable class: 9,000 tons (submerged). **L'Inflexible class:** 8,920 tons (submerged).
Dimensions: Length overall 420ft (128.0m); beam 34.8ft (10.6m); draught 32.8ft (10.0m).
Armament: Le Redoutable class: 16 M4 (*Le Redoutable* only) or 16 M20 (remaining boats) two-stage SLBMs; four 21in (533mm) tubes for 18 ECAN L5 Mod 3 or ECAN F17 Mod 2 torpedoes. **L'Inflexible class:** 16 M4 SLBMs; four 21in (533mm) tubes for SM 39 Exocet SSMs and/or ECAN L5 Mod 3 torpedoes (mixed SSM/torpedo load can be carried).
Propulsion: One pressurized water-cooled nuclear reactor, two steam-turbines (16,000bhp); one shaft; 20kts.

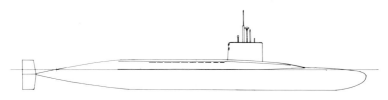

Above: A side elevation of one of five Le Redoutable class boats.

President De Gaulle decided in the early-1960s that France must have her own nuclear *force de dissuasion* and set the Navy the ambitious goal of developing both submarines and missiles from scratch, and with the absolute minimum of outside help. Unlike the British, the French had to work almost totally independently of the USA (although there was some covert assistance) and one consequence was that they had to develop SSBNs before SSNs. The whole

Below: *Le Redoutable* (S 611), the French Navy's first SSBN, was launched in March 1967 and was commissioned in December 1971. She is due to be retired from service during the early-1990s.

Above: A development of the Le Redoutable class, *L'Inflexible* (S 615) is armed with M4 SLBMs, SM 39 Exocet SSMs and up to 18 torpedoes.

Right: An impressive portrait of *Le Foudroyant* (S 610) heading out on patrol. One boat out of five is at sea at all times.

project involved a great national effort spread over a long period and was very expensive, but has proved to be a great success.

The first of class, *Le Redoutable* (S 611) was launched in 1967 and was followed by four others — *Le Terrible* (S 612), *Le Foudroyant* (S 610), *L'Indomptable* (S 613) and *Le Tonnant* (S 614), the last of which was launched in 1974. There was then a gap until it was decided to order a sixth boat, *L'Inflexible* (S 615), which was to be of an essentially similar design, but incorporating improvements in propulsion and electronics. She was also designed from the outset to carry the M4 missile. Externally, the sail is higher and more streamlined than on the earlier submarines, the hydroplanes are mounted higher and the "turtle-deck" forward of the sail is much more streamlined. She joined the fleet in 1985. All these SSBNs follow the general design criteria of other nations, with two rows of eight vertical SLBM tubes abaft the fin and a small number of conventional torpedo tubes for self-defence.

The M1 SLBM was fitted in the first two boats and had a range of 1,000nm (2.091nm). The improved M2 and the subsequent M20 missile were fitted into all Le Redoutable class SSBNs. The M20 has a single thermo-nuclear warhead with a 1.2 megaton yield, and a range of about 1,900nm (3,974km). An enlarged version, the M4 SLBM with six 150 kT MIRVs and a range of 2,900nm (6,114km), was tested in 1978-79 and has since been backfitted into all ships in the class with the exception of *Le Redoutable*.

Below: Note the higher setting of the hydroplanes on *L'Inflexible* (S 615) when compared with *Le Foudroyant* (S 610) at right.

Rubis Class

Fleet submarines
Six boats (S 601-S 606); two building (S 607-S 608).

Country of origin: France.
Displacement: 2,385 tons surfaced (2,400 tons S 605 onwards); 2,670 tons submerged.
Dimensions: Length overall 236.5ft (72.1m); beam 24.9ft (7.6m); depth 21ft (6.4m).
Armament: Four 21in (533mm) torpedo tubes; SNM 39 Exocet SSM; ECAN LS Mod 3 and ECAN F 17 Mod 2 torpedoes.
Propulsion: One pressurized water-cooled nuclear reactor, one electric motor (9500shp); 25 kts submerged.

Below: A bird's-eye view of *Rubis,* her progress slowed almost to a halt to enable the extraction of a crewman by a Lynx helicopter.

The French Navy first tried to acquire a nuclear-powered attack submarine in 1954, when feasibility studies were begun. In 1956 the first vessel was laid down, but political friction between France and the United States led the US to deny France the enriched uranium needed to fuel the reactor. France was then forced unsuccessfully to develop a heavy water reactor using natural uranium, which turned out to be too large and heavy for the planned submarine to carry.

A new development was started for the SSBN programme and the vital experience already gained enabled French constructors to produce an extremely compact integrated reactor which reduced the size of the propulsion plant, so enabling the Rubis class to be the smallest nuclear-powered submarine ever built.

Unlike the standard French diesel boats the Rubis has a single hull with bulkheads at each end. There are two decks for control and accommodation and the small area taken up by the nuclear reactor reduces the weight and space needed for shielding. These vessels can dive to 984ft (300m), and because of the discharge system employed torpedoes can be fired from any depth.

Rubis (S 601) entered service in February 1983, with 3 more boats (*Saphir* (S 602); *Casablanca* (S 603); *Emeraude* (S 604)) becoming operational by 1988. Four more vessels (*Amethyste* (S 605); *Perle* (S 606); *Turquoise* (S 607); *Diamant* (S 608)) have an increased length, a new bow form and a streamlined superstructure. This, coupled with a major silencing programme and new attack systems plus improved electronics will make for an effective force. The earlier boats are undergoing refits which should finish in 1995. A ninth boat of 4,000 tons is planned as the start of a new and improved type and should enter service early in the 21st Century, but delays in completing the Rubis class, because of economies imposed in 1989, may affect progress on this next group also.

Below: Bedecked in her national colours, *Amethyste* takes to the water for the first time on 14 May 1988. Her name is also an acronym for *Amelioration Tactique Hydrodynamique Silence Transmission Ecoute* (Reduced Radiation Emission).

Suffren (Type 66) Class

Guided-missile destroyers
Two ships (D 602-D 603).

Country of origin: France.
Displacement: 6,780 tons full load.
Dimensions: Length overall 517.1ft (157.6m); beam 50.9ft (15.5m); draught 20.0ft (6.1m).
Armament: One Masurca SAM system; four MM38 Exocet SSM launchers; two 3.9in (100mm) Model 1964 DP guns; four 0.8in (20mm) AA guns; one Malafon ASW system; two catapults for L 5 torpedoes.
Propulsion: Two sets Rateau geared turbines (72.500shp); two shafts; 34kts.

In the 1930s the French Navy established a reputation for building handsome, fast, well-armed and highly efficient large destroyers. The Le Fantasque class, for example, were completed in 1933-34 and despite a displacement of 3,400 tons and the heavy armament of five 5.5in (140mm) guns were capable of an astonishing 45.03kts, which must have been a very imposing sight! After the war some small and rather ugly destroyers were built, but then Gallic flair gave rise to a return to a more traditional concept with the Suffren class (Type F 60), the first of a new generation of French warships and also the first French purpose-built guided-missile destroyers.

These two ships, *Suffren* (D 602) and *Duquesne*(D 603), are large and elegant,

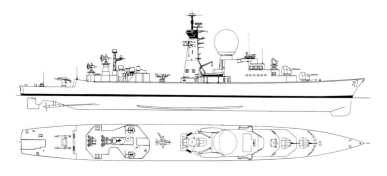

Above: The outline form of a 6,780-ton Suffren class destroyer.

and heavily armed. They mount two single 3.9in (100mm) guns forward, a Malafon ASW launcher immediately abaft the prominent mack (combined mast and stack), four MM 38 Exocet launchers on the after superstructure, a Masurca SAM launcher on the quarterdeck and a prominent variable-depth sonar (VDS) at the stern.

Below: Seen cruising off the French Riviera is *Suffren* (D 602). The enormous radome houses the DRBI-23 three-dimensional radar which provides air search and target designation data for the ship's Masurca air defence weapons system. On the foredeck is a pair of 3.9in (100mm) Model 1964 automatic guns.

These ships are immediately recognizable by their enormous glassfibre dome on top of the bridge which covers the DRBI 23 three-dimensional radar. The Suffrens are excellent seaboats and are good weapons platforms, rolling and pitching only slightly and having very little vibration. The use of a mack has also increased the available deck space for other weapons systems. A comprehensive selection of radar and ECM aerials are carried on the fore part of the mack. The Malafon ASMs provide long-range ASW defence and mean that a helicopter with its associated pad and hangar need not be carried.

The three-ship Tourville (Type F 67) class combined the best features of the

Above: Well-proportioned and well-designed, these destroyers enjoy excellent stability qualities — an important asset when it comes to weapons firing. Shown here is *Suffren* (D 602), as one of her 48 ECAN Ruelle Masurca SAMs takes to the air.

Suffren design with those of the smaller, earlier, anti-submarine Aconit (Type C 65) class. Still powered by geared turbines, they have a helicopter pad and hangar aft in place of the Masurca SAM. The Tourvilles have themselves been succeeded in production by the Type F 70 class (q.v.).

Gepard/Albatros (Type 143/A/B) Classes

Guided-missile patrol boats
20 craft: **Type 143/143B** — 10 (P 6111-P 6120); **Type 143A** — 10 (P 6121-P 6130).

Country of origin: Germany.
Displacement: Type 143/143B — 393 tons; **Type 143A** — 393.6 tons.
Dimensions: Length overall 189ft (57.6m); beam 25.5ft (7.76m); draught **Type 143/143B** — 9.25ft (2.82m), **Type 143A** — 9.8ft (2.99m).
Armament: Type 143/143B — Four MM 38 Exocet SSM launchers; two OTO Melara DP guns; two 21in (533mm) torpedo tubes. **Type 143A** — Four MM 38 Exocet SSM launchers; one RAM launcher; one 3in (76mm) OTO Melara DP gun; two minerails.
Propulsion: Four MTU 16V956 diesels (16,000bhp); four shafts; 36kts.

Lürssen's first post-war work was a series of patrol boats based on their highly effective Second World War *Schnellboote* design. These were developed into the Type 141 and Type 142 torpedo boats, built between 1957 and 1963. Meanwhile, Lürssen had developed a general-purpose hull which could be fitted with various engines and armaments, depending on the requirements of the purchasing navy. This design was produced by CMN, at Cherbourg in France, as the La Combattante (Type 148).

A scaled-up version of this design became the basis of a missile-armed patrol boat, the Type 143, 10 of which were constructed for the German Navy between 1972 and 1977. Intended for Baltic operations, they have a high speed and are fitted with two OTO Melara 3in (76mm) Compacts to ensure adequate anti-aircraft protection. An AG15 automatic data link with the shore base can be used for remote firing and control of their MM 38 Exocet SSMs. The Type 143s also carry two torpedo tubes firing *Seal* wire-guided torpedoes.

Ten further boats were built between 1979 and 1984 as the Type 143A. These are very similar to the Type 143, but are fitted for the Rolling Airframe Missile (RAM) close-in defence system, a much-delayed collaborative project with the USA, which should enter service in 1992/93. This replaces the aft 3in (76mm) gun and mine-rails are fitted instead of torpedo tubes.

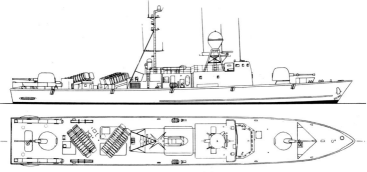

Above: The angled launchers for Exocet SSMs are clearly visible.

Above: The long tube on the stern port-side of *Bussard* (P6114) is a 21in (533mm) launch tube for Seal wire-guided torpedoes.

Left: The prominent cylindrical housing atop this Albatros class boat contains a Hollandsee-built radar.

Below: Another view of *Bussard* (P 6114), this time at speed in the Baltic Sea. Maximum speed is 36kts on 16,000bhp.

MEKO Class

Destroyers

12 ships: **Argentina** — four; **Nigeria** — one; **Portugal** — three; **Turkey** — four; (plus 14 building): **Australia** — eight; **Greece** — four; **New Zealand** — two.

Country of origin: Germany.
Displacement: 3,000 tons full load.
Dimensions: Length overall 362.5ft (110.5m); beam 43.6ft (13.3m); draught 12.8ft (3.9m).
Aircraft: One ASW helicopter (type varies).
Armament: Eight Harpoon SSM launchers; one Mk 29 launcher for Sea Sparrow SAMs; one 5in (127mm) Mk 45 DP gun; four 1in (25mm) GM Sea Zenith CIWS; six 12.7in (324mm) torpedo tubes.
Propulsion: Four MTU 20V1163 diesels (22,536shp); 27kts.
(Specifications are for Turkish MEKO 200; others differ in dimensions and weapons fit.)

One of the major dilemmas in modern naval construction is that warships are becoming ever more expensive and complex, while the growing size and ambitions of the world's smaller navies means that they want more of the latest types of warship — but within a limited budget. Several designers have, therefore, sought to produce warships of destroyer/frigate size which could accommodate a variety of weapons and electronic fits to suit different customers' needs on a common hull, which would result in longer production runs and reduced costs.

The basis of the MEKO concept, developed by Blohm & Voss in Germany, is a range of standard hulls, complemented by the MEKO/FES range of standard-sized, functionally self-contained modules with standard interfaces to the ship platform. Weapon functional units are used for the installation of guns, missile launchers and ASW rocket launchers. These units are bedded into a unit foundation using a plastic resin compound which transfers the static and dynamic loads to the ship's structure. Among the units on offer are Otomat SAMs, Aspide SSMs, 5in (127mm) guns and twin 1.6in (40mm) Breda AA guns, but the system is so flexible that almost anything could be handled.

Largest in the current range is the MEKO 360, a general-purpose destroyer designed for world-wide operations under all climatic conditions. Five of these are in service: four with Argentina (*Almirante Brown, La Argentina, Heroina* and *Sarandi*), and one with Nigeria (*Aradu*).

The slightly smaller MEKO 200 is proving more popular. Four are already in service with the Turkish Navy (*Yavuz, Turgut Reis, Fatih* and *Yildirim*), of which two were built in Germany and two in Turkey, and another three joined the Portuguese fleet in 1990-91 (*Vasco da Gama, Alvares Cabral*, and *Corte Real*). A further 14 are now under construction for three other navies: Australia — eight; Greece — four; and New Zealand — two.

The German Navy has recently ordered a new class of large destroyer — the Type 123. This will displace 4,275 tons and is being constructed by a consortium led by Blohm & Voss. This design is somewhat larger than the current MEKO range, but uses the Blohm & Voss modular construction techniques developed for the MEKO ships and will clearly benefit greatly from the experience gained with these foreign orders. Meanwhile the MEKO destroyers must rank as some of the most successful designs currently in service.

Below: Commissioned on 26 January 1983, *Almirante Brown* (D 10) was sent to the Gulf in late-1990 to support Allied operations.

Aster, Eridan and Alkmaar Classes

Coastal minehunters
35 ships: **Belgium** — 10 (M 915-M 924); **France** — 10 ships (M 641-M 650); **Netherlands** — 15 ships (M 850-M 864).

Countries of origin: Belgium, France and The Netherlands.
Displacement: 562 tons standard (595 full load).
Dimensions: Length overall 168.9ft (51.5m); beam 29.2ft (8.9m); draught 8.2ft (2.5m).
Armament: One DCN 0.8in (20mm) AA gun.
Propulsion: One diesel (2,280hp); one shaft; two manoeuvring propellers; bow thruster.
(Specifications and data are for Aster class).

In the event of war it is evident that both sides in a conflict will employ a large number of mines to create maximum havoc amongst opposing forces. The Western powers have somewhat neglected the development of mines since the Second World War; in contrast the Soviet Union has an impressive record in this sphere and the means of deploying them. The West countered this threat with a range of hunters each country responding with its own type, but at the end of the 1970s Belgium, France and the Netherlands entered into an agreement to build a new class of 35 vessels. A "ship factory" was built at Ostend in Belgium, with the hulls being towed to Rupelmonde for fitting out. Each country builds its own hulls but France supplies all the MCM gear and electronics. Belgium supplies the electrical installation and the Netherlands is responsible for the supply of engine room equipment. The hulls are fitted with tank stabilization, and there is full NBC protection and air-conditioning. They have two manoeuvering propellers and a bow thruster. A 5-ton container housing various stores for use in the HQ support, patrol, extended diving and drone control tasks is carried. Range is 2,540nm (4,826km) at 12kts.

Detail discussions were started in 1989 between Belgium and the Netherlands for a combined project to build 14 600-ton minehunters, the first of which is to be laid down in 1993. They are planned to have a range of 2,540nm (4,826km)

Below: One of the 15 Alkmaar class minehunters in service with the Royal Netherlands Navy is *Haarlem* (M 853), shown here while on exercise in the North Sea.

at a sweep speed of 10kts, and the ability to sweep bottom mines which have sunk deep into the soft sand of the southern section of the North Sea, rendering them difficult to detect by existing methods.

The Western powers now pay great attention to mine-hunting as mine-laying in the areas around the coast of Northern Europe would pay huge dividends in seas often les than 200ft (60m) deep. The entire North Sea, Atlantic approaches to Europe and the English Channel lie above this depth and sea traffic is often forced to use restricted channels owing to shoals and banks. Such an area is ideal for offensive mine-laying, especially in channels used by SSBN and SSN submarines entering or leaving their home bases.

Below: In contrast to the 10 Belgian Aster class minehunters, the French Eridan class (the first of which, *Eridan* (M 641), is illustrated) and the Dutch Alkmaar class vessels each sport a single GIAT 20F2 0.8in (20mm) gun on the foredeck.

Audace Class

Destroyers
Two ships: D 550-D 551.

Country of origin: Italy.
Displacement: 4,554 tons.
Dimensions: Length 461.6ft (140.7m); beam 48.1in (14.65m); draught 15.1ft (4.6m).
Aircraft: One Sikorsky SH-3D Sea King or two Agusta-Bell AB.212ASW helicopters.
Armament: Eight OTOMAT-Teseo SSM launchers; one Mk 13 missile launcher for Standard SM-1MR SAM; one Albatros SAM system; one 5in (127mm) OTO Melara Compact DP gun; four OTO Melara 3in (76mm) Super-Rapid DP guns; four 21in (533mm) torpedo tubes; six 12.7in (324mm) ASW torpedo tubes.
Propulsion: Two sets geared turbines (73,000shp); SEMT-Pielstick 12 PC 2 V400 diesels; two shafts; 33kts.
(Specifications are for post-modernization weapons fits.)

Below: An outline of Italy's Audace class destroyer. Only two of these well-armed vessels have been constructed to date.

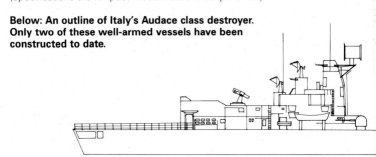

The Impectuoso class, the first post-war destroyers to be designed and built in Italy, were ordered in 1950, and were strongly influenced by American designs. Flush-decked and twin-funnelled, they were armed with American guns and fitted with American radar and sonar.

The next class, the Impavidos ordered in 1957 and 1959, were enlarged and improved versions with the aft 5in mount replaced by a single Mk 13 Tartar SAM launcher capable of launching Tartar or Standard missiles. There is magazine space for 40 missiles. The 1.6in (40mm) guns were replaced by the Italian Brescia 3in (76mm) gun.

The Audace class is a further enlargement and development of the Impavidos, with a slightly larger hull. The US 5in (127mm) guns were replaced by two single, superposed 5in (127mm) OTO Melara guns, but in a late-1980s refit one of these was replaced by an Albatros SAM system, which comprises an OTO Melara launcher and Aspide missiles (Italian versions of the Sea Sparrow). Long-range air defence is provided by Standard SAMs, for which one Mk 13 launcher is provided, located just forward of the hangar, atop the 40-round magazine. The large hangar can accommodate two Agusta-Bell AB.212ASWs or a single Sikorsky SH-3D Sea King (or, in the future, one Agusta-Westland EH.101 Merlin). The ships have a comprehensive fit of US, Dutch and Italian radars, but, somewhat surprisingly, have steam- rather than gas-powered turbines.

Bottom: Seen cutting through the waters of the Mediterranean Sea is *Audace* (D 551). Although assigned the higher of the two pennant numbers, *Audace* was commissioned ahead of sistership *Ardito* (D 550), in November 1972.

Giuseppe Garibaldi

Light fleet carrier
One carrier (C 551).

Country of origin: Italy.
Displacement: 10,100 tons standard (13,370 tons full load).
Dimensions: Length overall 591ft (180m); flight deck length 570.2ft (173.8m); beam 110.2ft (33.4m); draught 22ft (6.7m).
Aircraft: 16 McDonnell Douglas AV-8B Harrier II fighters; 18 Sikorsky SH-3D Sea King AEW/ASW helicopters.
Armament: Four OTO Melara missile launchers, two Selenia octuple launchers; six Breda 1.6in (40mm) guns. Six 12.7in (324mm) torpedo tubes firing Honeywell Mk 46 anti-submarine torpedoes.
Propulsion: Four Fiat gas turbines (80,000hp); 30 knots.

Below: A 6.5deg ski-jump set in the bows of the *Giuseppi Garibaldi* will enable AV-8B Harrier IIs to take off at higher gross weights. Up to 16 of these potent VSTOL fighters will be carried.

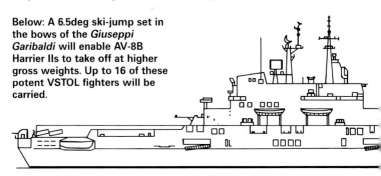

Below: A fine view of the integral ski-jump aboard the *Giuseppi Garibaldi,* with Royal Navy Sea Harriers on deck for launch trials.

Giuseppe Garibaldi is the first aircraft carrier to enter service with the Italian Navy. Previous examples utilizing converted liners during the Second World War were scuttled before they could be completed.

Authorized in late-1977, design work was not completed until early-1980 owing to extensive design changes. Laid down in March 1981, launched in June 1983 and commissioned in August 1987, the carrier has six decks with 13 water-tight bulkheads. A 6.5deg ski-jump for VSTOL aircraft forms part of the forward flight-deck, which in turn is served by two lifts leading to a 361ft x 49.2ft x 19.7ft (110m x 15m x 6m) hangar. By 1993, 16 AV-8B Harriers will be carried plus 18 SH-3D Sea King helicopters (twelve in the hangar and six on deck). Later these will be replaced by EH. 101s. The long-standing dispute between the Navy and Air Force concerning the former's operation of fixed-wing aircraft dates back prior to the Second World War and was not clarified until 1989, when it was decided that embarked aircraft were purchased and operated by the Navy with the Air Force providing maintenance, any evaluation and additional pilots if needed.

The first group of Navy pilots were trained in 1990-91 by the US Marine Corps. All defence is provided by six Breda 1.6in (40mm) AA guns plus four Melara active radar homing missiles and two Selenia Elsag Albatros octuple launchers with an envelope from only 49.2ft (15m) to 16,405ft (5,000m). There are also two triple torpedo mounts for anti-submarine defence.

Giuseppe Garibaldi has a range of 7000nm (13,300km) at 20kts.

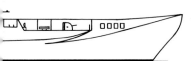

Below: A view of the *Giuseppi Garibaldi's* stern reveals one of the trio of Breda 1.6in (40mm) double-barrelled guns for anti-air and anti-surface defensive fire. Rate-of-fire is 300 rounds-per-minute, with an elevation of 85deg.

Maestrale Class

Guided missile frigates
Eight ships (F 570-F 577).

Country of origin: Italy.
Displacement: 3,060 tons full load.
Dimensions: Length overall 402.6ft (122.7m); beam 42.3ft (12.9m); draught 13.5ft (4.1m).
Aircraft: Two Agusta-Bell AB.212ASW helicopters.
Armament: Four Teseo-Automat Mk 2 SSM launchers; one Albatros SAM system; one 5in (127mm) OTO Melara DP gun; four 1.6in (40mm) Breda Dardo AA mounts; two 21in (533mm) torpedo tubes; six 12.7in (324mm) ILAS-3 ASW torpedo tubes.
Propulsion: CODOG. Two General-Electric-Fiat LM-2500 gas turbines (50,000shp); two GMT B 230-20 BVM diesels (10.146bhp); two shafts; 33kts.

Italy produced the successful Lupo class frigates between 1974 and 1980. With a displacement of 2,525 tons, they are heavily armed for their size and also carry an AB.212ASW helicopter, for which they are fitted with a telescopic hangar. Four were bought by the Italian Navy, six by Venezuela, four by Peru and four by Iraq (although the latter have not yet reached that country, due to financial and political problems). Like so many Italian ship designs they have a very high top speed, the nameship of the class, *Lupo*, having attained no less than 35.23kts during trials.

It was then decided to construct an enlarged version — the Maestrale class. This is some 30ft (9.2m) longer and with a 5ft (1.54m) increase in beam, resulting in a 675 tons greater displacement and a loss of about 2.5kts in top speed. Four SSM launch tubes have been removed to enable the hangar to accommodate two AB.212ASW helicopters to the Lupos' one. The flight-deck is also larger, being 88.6ft (27m) long and 39.4ft (12m) wide.

There is a stern-well for a new Variable Depth Sonar (VDS) which is streamed on a 1.968ft (600m) cable. There are plans to increase the capability of this system by extending the cable to 2,952ft (900m). It is also planned to attach a towed, passive hydrophone array to the VDS "fish".

Below: *Scirocco* (F 573), the fourth Maestrale class frigate, displays her prominent stern-mounted helicopter landing pad.

The first ship was commissioned in 1982 and the eighth and last in 1985; so far, unlike the Lupo class, no export orders have been received. The ships in the class are: *Maestrale, Grecale, Libeccio, Scirocco, Aliseo, Euro, Espero* and *Zeffiro*.

There will be a need to replace the four Lupo class frigates at the end of this decade and the Italian Navy had planned to procure the NFR 90 (NATO Frigate Replacement 90) to fill this requirement. With the collapse of the NFR 90, however, the most likely course will be to built for more of the Maestrale class, although the design, weapon and electronics would, of course, be updated.

Below: The foredeck of the Maestrale class is dominated by the 5in (127mm) OTO Melara gun, with an 85deg elevation.

Sparviero Class

Guided-missile hydrofoils
Seven ships (P 420-P 427).

Country of origin: Italy.
Displacement: 62.5 tons full load.
Dimensions: *Hull:* length overall 75.3ft (23m); beam 22.9in (7m); draught
4.3ft (1.3m). *Foils down:* length overall 80.7ft (24.6m); beam 39.7ft (12.1m);
draught (*hull-borne*) 14.4ft (4.4m); draught (*foil-borne*) 4.3ft (1.3m).
Armament: Two Otomat 2 SSMs in single launchers; one 3in (76mm) gun
in single mounting.
Propulsion: One Rolls-Royce Proteus gas-turbine driving water-jet
(4500bhp); one diesel; maximum speed 52kts.

In the early-1960s the Americans built three experimental hydrofoil patrol
boats. These were tested for several years, then between 1966 and 1968
two competitive patrol hydrofoils were built. *Flagstaff* (PGH-1), built by
Grumman, was a conventional surface-piercing hydrofoil with two struts
forward and one aft. *Tucumcari* (PGH-2), based on the previous *High Point*
(PCH-1), adopted her fully submerged foil system. This uses one strut
forward and two aft. It is inherently unstable, and when foil-borne relies on a
small computer and a wave-height sensing system to keep the foils
submerged and hull clear of the water. The foils can be retracted for cruising.
Tucumcari (PGH-2) displaced 58 tons light, and was armed at one
time with one 1.6in (40mm) and two twin 0.5in (12.7mm) machine-guns and
one 3.2in (81mm) mortar. Powered by one Rolls-Royce Proteus gas-turbine with
water-jets when foil-borne, and a General Motors diesel for cruising, she had
a foil-borne speed of over 40kts. She was discarded in 1973, but in her five
years of trials operated successfully in Sea State 6, despite being designed
for Sea State 4. *Sparviero* (P 420) is an improved version of *Tucumcari*

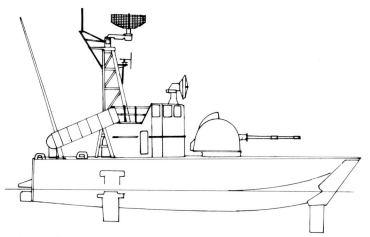

Above: Note the Sparvieros' extended foils and 3in (76mm) gun.

with a slightly larger hull and greatly improved armament. She was designed and built by Alinavi, a consortium of Boeing, the Italian government and the Italian commercial hydrofoil builder Carlo Rodriguez. She was intended as the basis for a NATO hydrofoil, but nine of this class were authorized for the Italian Navy in the 1975 *Legge Navale*. She is well suited for short-range operations in the Mediterranean, and has successfully fired Otomat Mk 1 SSMs, which have an effective range of over 31.3nm (59.5km). Seven hydrofoils are in commission and are used for short-range missions, as no berths are fitted for the crewmen.

Below: A fine study of *Sparviero* (P 420) on a high-speed run.

Vittorio Veneto Class

Guided-missile helicopter cruiser
One ship (C 550).

Country of origin: Italy.
Displacement: 9,500 tons full load.
Dimensions: Length overall 589.2ft (179.6m); beam 63.7ft (19.42); draught 18.0ft (5.5m).
Aircraft: Six Agusta-Bell AB.212ASW helicopters.
Armament: One Mk 10 Aster launcher for Standard SM-1 MR SAMs and ASROC ASW missiles; four Otomat/Teseo SSM launchers; eight OTO Melara 3in (76mm) Compact DP guns; six 1.6in (40mm) Breda Dardo AA guns; six 12.7in (324mm) ASW torpedo tubes.
Propulsion: Two sets Tosi geared turbines (73,000shp); two shafts; 30.5kts.

In the early-1960s the Italian Navy built two helicopter-carrying cruisers, *Andrea Doria* and *Caio Duilio*, which combined a heavy armament forward with a large flightdeck and hangar aft providing accommodation for up to three AB.212 helicopters. When the time came for a successor, two designs were proposed. One was for a large ship capable of being used for amphibious assault as well as for ASW, which would probably have resembled the French *Jeanne d'Arc*. The other, successful design was for a larger and more refined *Andrea Doria*, which emerged as the *Vittorio Veneto* (C 550). Like the *Andrea Doria* she has a twin launcher forward (Mark 10), which can launch Standard SM-1 MR SAMs or ASROC ASW missiles. She has eight OTO Melara 3in (76mm) AA guns in four twin mounts arranged around the superstructure. By installing macks (com-

bined masts and stacks) deck space has been saved in order to accommodate a much larger flight-deck than on the Andrea Doria class, with the hangar below

The *Vittorio Veneto* is a very effective vessel, ideally suited to ASW operations in Mediterranean conditions. Until the commissioning of *Giuseppe Garibaldi*, *Vittorio Veneto* was the largest ship in the Italian Navy and was always used as the official flagship.

Above: The sole vessel in her class, *Vittorio Veneto* officially serves the Italian Navy as a guided-missile helicopter cruiser.

Below: The spacious helipad astern indicates the importance the Italian Navy places on a rotary-winged ASW capability. Up to six Agusta-Bell AB.212ASW helicopters can be accommodated.

Chikugo Class

Frigates

11 ships including *Chikugo* (DE-215); *Teshio* (DE-222).

Country of origin: Japan
Displacement: 1470-1500 tons (1700-1730 full load).
Dimensions: Length overall 305·5ft (93·1m); beam 35·5ft (10·8m); draught 11·5ft (3·5m).
Armament: Two 3in (76mm) guns in twin mounting, two 40mm AA guns in twin mounting; one ASROC Mk16 octuple launcher; two triple Mk32 torpedo tubes.
Propulsion: Four diesels (16,000shp), twin shafts; 25kts.

The first Japanese postwar frigates were Japanese and American World War II destroyer escorts. Both steam and diesel propulsion were tried in the

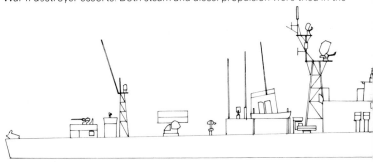

Haruna Class

Helicopter destroyers

Two ships: *Haruna* (DD 141); *Hiei* (DD 142).

Country of origin: Japan.
Displacement: 4700 tons.
Dimensions: Length overall 502ft (153m); beam 57·4ft (17·5m); draught 16·7ft (5·1m).
Aircraft: Three Sikorsky H-SS2 helicopters.
Armament: Two 5in (127mm) guns in single mounts; ASROC octuple Mk16 launcher; two triple US Mk32 torpedo tubes.
Propulsion: Two geared turbines (70,000shp), twin shafts; 32kts.

The Japanese Maritime Self Defence Force is limited to a purely defensive function, and as a result it has not been permitted to build any major warship that might be used in an offensive role. Therefore, unlike other helicopter

Left: *Haruna* fires an ASROC anti-submarine missile. Designed for a purely defensive role, she has a heavy anti-submarine armament.

1953 programme escorts, but steam power was abandoned in the subsequent *Isuzu* class, built between 1960 and 1964. These were flush decked diesel powered frigates of 1,490 tons (1,510 tonnes) standard displacement armed with a twin 3in (76mm) mount fore and aft. The first pair have a single Weapon Able A/S rocket-launcher in B position, with a four-barrel 12in (305mm) rocket-launcher, while the second pair have a triple-barrel Bofors 14·75in (375mm) A/S rocket-launcher and six A/S torpedo tubes. They have hull-mounted sonar, with VDS in two ships. The *Chikugo* class were developed from the *Isuzus*, but have an ASROC A/S launcher and bow and variable depth sonar. They have a much larger bridge, and the ASROC launcher is mounted just aft of the funnel. Their twin 3in (76mm) mount is forward of the bridge and the twin 40mm mount is at the stern, just forward of the variable depth sonar. The later members of the class incorporated minor improvements. A larger version, the *Yamagumo/Minegumo* class destroyers, built since 1964, have a standard displacement of 2150 tons (2184 tonnes) and a speed of 27kts. They have a very similar armament to the *Isuzus* and *Chikugos*, but the second group had a landing pad and hangar for DASH helicopters, which were replaced by ASROC in 1977. The frigates are too small to carry a helicopter and a balanced anti-aircraft and anti-submarine amament, but like all postwar Japanese warships they operate within range of land-based anti-submarine aircraft.

Left: *Chikugo*. The eleven frigates of the Chikugo class are the smallest warships in the world to mount ASROC. Like all other Japanese Maritime Defence Force ships they are designed to fight under shore-based air cover and thus have light air defence systems.

equipped destroyers and cruisers. the *Haruna* class have been optimised for the anti-submarine role, with a very limited anti-aircraft and surface capability. This has, however, meant that the *Harunas* carry virtually the same anti-submarine armament as the Italian *Andrea Doria* helicopter cruisers on 1,300 tons (1,320 tonnes) less standard displacement. *Haruna* carries her two 5in (127mm) Mk 42 guns in single mounts, forward, with the ASROC launcher between B gun and the massive bridge. The uptakes are arranged in a mack which is surmounted by a lattice mast. The hangar, which can accommodate three HHS-2 helicopters, is an integral part of the superstructure. The flight deck stretches the entire aft third of the ship. The Mk 32 torpedo tubes are in two triple mounts one on either side of the bridge. The armament and much of the equipment is American, as with all postwar Japanese ships. Two improved *Harunas*, the *Shirane* class, have been built. These go far towards remedying the *Harunas'* deficiencies in anti-aircraft armament, having a BPDM Sea Sparrow SAM launcher and two twin 35mm anti-aircraft guns in addition to the *Haruna's* armament. They are slightly larger, having a standard displacement of 5,200 tons (5,280 tonnes).

Below: *Haruna*. Two 5in (127mm) guns and ASROC are before the bridge. Large hangar and long flight-deck are aft.

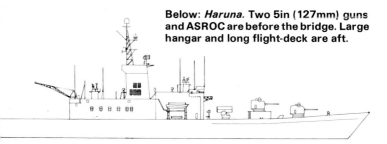

Kortenaer Class

Frigates

20 ships: **Netherlands** — 10 (F 807-F 811, F 816, F 823-F 826); **Germany** — eight (F 207-F 214); **Greece** — two (F 450-F 451).

Country of origin: The Netherlands.
Displacement: 3,786 tons full load.
Dimensions: Length overall 427.2ft (130.2m); beam 47.2ft (14.4m); draught 14.3ft (4.4m).
Aircraft: Two Westland Lynx ASW helicopters.
Armament: Four Harpoon SSM launchers; one NATO Sea Sparrow SAM system; one 3in (76mm) OTO Melara DP gun; one 1.12in (30mm) Goalkeeper CIWS; four 12.7in (324mm) torpedo tubes.
Propulsion: CODOG. Two Rolls-Royce Olympus TM-38 gas turbines (50,000shp); two Rolls-Royce Tyne RM-1C gas turbines (8,000shp); two shafts; 30kts.

Between 1975 and 1983 the Royal Netherlands Navy undertook a fundamental reorganization in which it created an integrated and balanced force consisting of three ASW task groups in war. Each would comprise a flagship/air defence ship, six ASW frigates and a logistic support vessel and would be allocated to NATO. To achieve this a new class of frigates was required to augment and eventually replace the Van Speijk class, which were Dutch-built versions of the British Leander class. The result was the Kortenaer class, which has proved an outstanding success.

Displacing 3,786 tons, the Kortenaer is one of the larger classes in service and is well armed. For surface warfare there are four Harpoon SSM launchers (a further four can be carried in war) and a single 3in (76mm) OTO Melara DP gun, one of the most widely used naval guns in the world. Air defence weapons comprise the NATO Sea Sparrow system, for which 29 missiles are carried, and

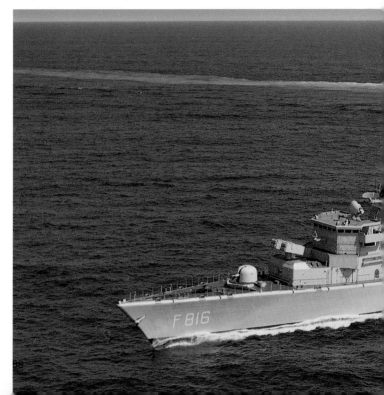

a Dutch-designed Goalkeeper 1.12in (30mm) CIWS (not yet fitted to all ships in the class). For the ASW mission a large hangar can accommodate two Westland Lynx helicopters, although in peacetime only one is normally carried.

Germany has built eight of these ships as the Bremen (Type 122) class, which are generally similar to the Dutch ships but are modified for operations in the Baltic Sea and are powered by GE-Fiat gas turbines and MTU diesels, in a CODOG arrangement. The Greek Navy operates two Dutch-built ships as the Elli class, which have slightly lengthened hangars to enable them to accommodate the Agusta-Bell AB.212ASW helicopter, which they use instead of the Westland Lynx.

Above: The Royal Netherlands Navy frigate *Kortenaer* (F 807), one of 10 such ships currently operated by this NATO member.

Below: A fine study of *Abraham Crijnssen* (F 816), the sixth example of the Kortenaer class to join the Royal Netherlands Navy, as she demonstrates her very impressive manoeuvreability at speed.

Tromp Class

Guided-missile destroyers
Two ships (F 801-F 806).

Country of origin: The Netherlands.
Displacement: 4,308 tons full load.
Dimensions: Length overall 453.4ft (138.2m); beam 48.6ft (14.8m); draught 15.1ft (4.6m).
Aircraft: One Westland Lynx helicopter.
Armament: Four Harpoon SSM launchers; one Mk 13 launcher for Standard SM-1 MR SAMs; one NATO Sea Sparrow SAM system; two 4.7in (120mm) Bofors DP guns; six 21in (533mm) torpedo tubes.
Propulsion: COGOG. Two Rolls-Royce Olympus TM-3B gas-turbines (54,000shp); two Rolls-Royce Tyne RM-1C gas turbines (8,200shp); two shafts; 30kts.

The Dutch destroyers *Tromp* (F 801) and *De Ruyter* (F 806) entered service in 1975-76, replacing two De Zeven Provincien class cruisers. They combine the roles of task group flagship with that of air defence ship, the principle air defence system being the Standard SM-1 MR, whose Mk 13 launcher is located aft, just forward of the hangar. Close-in protection is afforded by the Sea Sparrow SAM system, whose launcher is mounted in the 'B' gun position. Atop the bridge is a very large glass-fibre dome covering the Dutch SPS-01 3-D air search radar, which gave these two ships their nickname of the "Kojak class."

Long-range surface warfare is conducted with Harpoon SSMs; there are normally four launchers between the bridge and stacks, but this can be increased to eight in war. The twin 4.7in (120mm) guns came from scrapped Holland class destroyers, but were thoroughly modernized prior to installation.

The primary ASW system is a single Westland Lynx helicopter, with a hangar and flightdeck aft. There are also two triple Mk 32 torpedo tubes, one set mounted either side of the after superstructure.

These ships are powered by gas-turbines in a COGOG arrangement, Rolls-Royce Olympuses being used for full speed and Rolls-Royce Tynes for cruising.

Above: *Tromp* (F 801) exercising in the North Sea. The massive and highly distinctive radome atop the superstructure houses a Hollandse Signaalapparaten three-dimensional Multiple-Target Tracking Radar. Note also the very large bridge.

Below: Appropriately nicknamed the "Kojak class", *Tromp* (F 801) and her sistership *De Ruyter* (F 806) sport an impressive array of weaponry. Immediately aft of the foredeck 4.7in (120mm) gun is the octuple launcher for 16 Sea Sparrow Mk 29 SAMs.

Aist Class

Air-cushion vehicles
20 craft.

Country of origin: Soviet Union.
Displacement: 220 tons.
Dimensions: Length 156.8ft (47.8m); beam 57.4ft (17.5m).
Armament: Four 1.12in (30mm) AK-230 CIWS.
Propulsion: Two gas-turbines (24,000shp); 4 propellers; two lift fans; 70kts.

The Soviet Navy has shown itself to be very eager to seize upon and develop new ideas, in marked contrast to the normal conservatism of the Russian character. They have, therefore, been in the forefront of air-cushion vehicle (ACV) development, with over 70 in service. Twenty 15-ton Lebed class ACVs have

been in service since 1967 and these small craft paved the way for the 27-ton Gus class, which is designed to carry 24 Soviet marines on amphibious operations. These ACVs are powered by three 780shp gas-turbines, two for propulsion and one for lift.

The impressive Aist class appeared in 1971, specifically designed for naval use, carrying either four PT-76 light tanks plus 50 marines, or two medium tanks (e.g. T-54/55s) and 200 marines. Twenty are known to be in service, together with five of the even more powerful Pomornik class, the first of which entered service in 1986.

These ACVs were built at the height of the Cold War and their role was clearly intended to be the transportation of Soviet marines on rapid attacks against NATO coastal targets. Now that the Cold War is over and the Soviet Union is in a state of turmoil, their role is much less clear.

Below: Nowhere has the British invention of the hovercraft been embraced more eagerly and effectively than in the Soviet Navy.

Below: This *Gus* class ACV is a naval version of the 50-seat *Skate* class.

Akula Class

Fleet submarines
Seven boats; six building.

Country of origin: Soviet Union.
Displacement: 7,500 tons surfaced (9,100 tons submerged).
Dimensions: Length overall 377.3ft (115m); beam 45.9ft (14m); depth 34.1ft (10.4m).
Armament: Four 21in (533mm) and four 25.6in (650mm) tubes; SS-N-21 SLCM; SS-N-15 and SS-N-16/-16B SSN; Type 53 and Type 65 torpedoes.
Propulsion: Two nuclear reactors; one shaft; 32kts submerged.

Launched in July 1984, *Akula* is the first of a large group of submarines that will follow on from the Victor III class. They are of a more traditional design with a broad hull and long, streamlined fin; the engineering standards on the bridge and casing are greater than on earlier classes; and improved underwater sen-

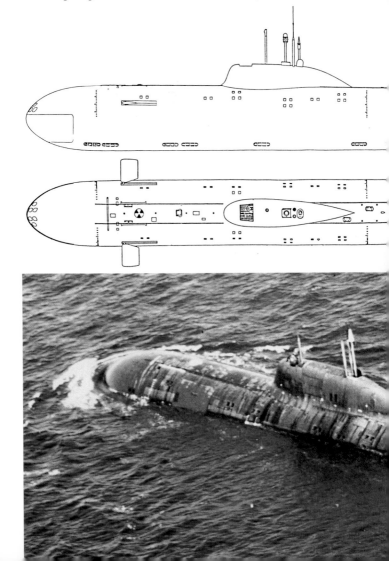

sors are fitted. These vessels also have a greatly reduced noise level which makes them harder to detect than the Victors.

The performance of the fleet submarine has been greatly increased with the introduction of the SS-N-21 tube-launched land attack missile with a range of 1,600nm (3,040km). *Akula* also carries a towed array dispenser which, although it has taken several years to develop, is thought not to be too effective.

Current plans call for two boats to be built per year. The existing vessels are based in the Northern and Pacific Fleets, where they serve alongside the very similar Sierra class; both types were developed at the same time and carry the same array of sensors. *Akula* was launched from the Komosomolk shipyard in the Pacific, whilst the first of the Sierras was built in the Western Soviet Union, so giving rise to a regional approach to the growing Soviet submarine fleet.

Standard anti-ship and acoustic homing torpedoes can be launched from the 21in (533mm) tubes, which can also fire SS-N-15 nuclear-tipped anti-submarine missiles as well as the SS-NX-21 cruise missiles; whilst the 25.6in (650mm) tubes are able to launch both the Type 65 torpedo, which has a range of 54nm (100km) and homes in on the wake of a surface ship, and the SS-N-16 torpedo-carrying anti-submarine missile.

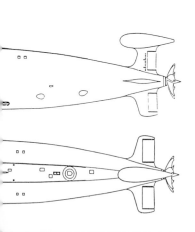

Left: One of the most visible distinguishing features of the Akula class is the long, low sail, quite unlike anything found on the West's SSNs. The large "teardrop" fairing atop the vertical rudder was first seen on the Victor III boats, and acts as a protective housing for a towed sonar array.

Below: An Akula class submarine caught on the surface by a US Navy maritime patrol aircraft, and recorded on film to add to the intelligence file held on this design. Having produced relatively small quantities of Akulas and Sierras, the former appears to have been selected for large-scale production.

Charlie I-II Classes

Nuclear-powered cruise-missile submarines
Charlie I — nine boats; **Charlie II** — six boats.

Country of origin: Soviet Union.
Displacement: 5,500 tons (**Charlie I** — 5,000 tons).
Dimensions: Length 337.9ft (103.0m) (**Charlie I** — 308.4ft (94.0m); beam 32.8ft (10.0m); draught 26.2ft (8.0m).
Armament: Eight SS-N-9 SLCM (**Charlie I** — eight SS-N-7 SLCM); six 21in (533mm) tubes for SS-N-15 torpedoes.
Propulsion: One pressurized water-cooled nuclear reactor; steam turbines; one shaft; 24kts.
(Specifications are for Charlie II; Charlie I is identical except where indicated.)

The shortcomings of the first Soviet cruise-missile submarines (SSGN) were readily apparent to the Soviet Navy and the next class to appear — the Charlie class — largely rectified them. Although the Charlies remain noisier than Western submarines, they are a major improvement on the Echos. They have a similar hull-form and machinery to the Victor class SSNs and have a similarly high submerged speed. The Charlie I was first seen by Western observers in 1968 and nine were produced before production switched to the longer Charlie II, of which six were built. All are believed still to be in service. One boat leased to India in 1988 was returned in early-1991.

They are fitted with eight missile tubes in the bow casing for SS-N-7 (Charlie I) or SS-N-9 missiles (Charlie II). The SS-N-7 is launched while the submarine is submerged and delivers a conventional warhead to a maximum range of 35nm (66.5km); speed is Mach 0.9. This missile is carried only by Charlie I class submarines, but the Charlie II weapon, the SS-N-9, is also carried by Nanuchka class missile boats. The SS-N-9 has inertial guidance and active radar homing, and a range of some 60nm (114km) if a forward observer with a video data link can be deployed. The missile normally carries a conventional warhead, but may also use a 200kT nuclear warhead.

Above: A Charlie I nuclear-powered cruise-missile submarine.

Above: A Charlie I SSGN, one of nine to be built before giving way to the updated Charlie II *et seq*. This initial model weighs in at 5,000 tons and totes eight SS-N-7 SLCMs.

The "one-off" Papa class SSGN appeared in 1970, armed with ten SS-N-9 SLCMs. Clearly a trials boat, it has rarely seen and may well now be out of Soviet Navy service.

Below: Development of the Charlie family of submarines finally saw Soviet naval designers making efforts to reduce underwater noise levels. Consequently, the Charlie's hull form is a great improvement on other designs, such as the Echo class.

Delta I-IV Classes

Nuclear-powered ballistic-missile submarines
Delta I — 18 boats; **Delta II** — four boats; **Delta III** — 14 boats; **Delta IV** — eight boats.

Country of origin: Soviet Union.
Displacement: 13,500 tons (**Delta I** — 11,300 tons; **Delta II** — 13,200 tons; **Delta III** — 13,250 tons).
Dimensions: Length 538.0ft (164.0m) (**Delta I** — 459.3ft (140.0m); **Delta II/III** — 510.2ft (155.5m); beam 39.4ft (12.0m); draught 28.2ft (8.6m).
Armament: 16 SS-N-23 SLBM (**Delta I** — 12 SS-N-8; **Delta II** — 16 SS-N-8; **Delta III** — 16 SS-N-18); six 21in (533mm) torpedo tubes.
Propulsion: Two pressurized water-cooled nuclear reactors, steam-turbines; 50,000shp; two shafts; 25kts.
(Specifications are for **Delta IV;** differences with **Deltas I, II** and **III** are as noted).

Up to 1973 the USA had a considerable advantage in the quality of their SLBMs, but in that year the Soviets introduced the SS-N-8, which, with a range of some 4,200nm (7,980km) outranged not only Poseidon but also Trident. Initial trials were made with a Hotel III submarine, but the missiles first became operational in the Delta I class, an improved and lengthened version of the Yankee class SSBN. As in the Yankee class, but unlike Western SSBNs, the Delta Is carried only 12

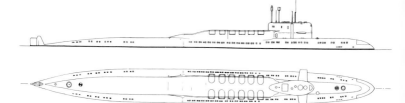

Above: The outline form of one of 18 Delta I SSBNs to be built.

missiles in two rows of six abaft the sail. Because the missiles are considerably longer than the diameter of the pressure hull the missile housing forms a "hump" above the outer casing.

Eighteen Delta Is entered service between 1972 and 1977, but a lengthened version — Delta II — carrying 16 SS-N-8s was already in production, four being commissioned between 1974-75. Then came the Delta III, using substantially the same hull as Delta II, but armed with 16 of the more modern SS-N-18; 14 joined the fleet between 1975 and 1982. These have an even higher housing for the missiles to accommodate the greater length of the SS-N-18.

Finally, in 1985 yet another version of the class appeared — Delta IV — with the even more advanced SS-N-23, SUBM.

Below: The large and distinctive box-like fairing abaft the fin is needed to safely accommodate the 12 large SS-N-8 missiles.

Ivan Rogov Class

Landing platform docks
Three ships.

Country of origin: Soviet Union.
Displacement: 11,000 tons (13,100 full load).
Dimensions: Length overall 521.6ft (159m); beam 80.2ft (24.5m); draught 21.2ft (6.5m).
Aircraft: Four Kamov Ka-29TB Helix-B combat transport helicopters.
Armament: One twin SA-N-4 SAM launcher; two SA-N-5/8 SAM systems; one twin 3in (76mm) gun mounting; four 0.9in (23mm) gatlings; one BM-21 (naval) rocket launcher.
Propulsion: Four diesels (20,000shp) 20kts.

One of the most remarkable expansions in capability by the Soviet Navy has been in amphibious warfare, but, because landing ships lack the glamour of destroyers or cruisers, this has passed largely unnoticed in the West.

The first major class was the Polnochniy landing craft tank (LCT) of which some 60 have been built. There are four groups within the class varying in full load displacement from 950-1,250 tons. They have a carrying capacity of six tanks. A further 23 Polnochniys have been built at Gdansk for Poland.

Next to appear were the 14 landing ships tank (LST) of the Alligator class, with a full load displacement of 4,500 tons. Commissioned in the late 'sixties these ships serve regularly in African and Asian waters, usually with Soviet marines embarked, and they represent a major extension of Soviet political and military power.

In a new departure, the Soviet Navy then ordered Ropucha class LSTs from Poland, thus, of course, releasing space in Soviet dockyards for other warship construction. The first such vessel was commissioned in 1975 and they have appeared at a rate of three-per-year since. The Ropuchas have a displacement of 4,400 tons full load and have greater personnel accommodation than the Alligators.

In 1978 the *Ivan Rogov* appeared; this is a 13,000-ton LPD of novel and sensible design. It was quite clearly intended to project Soviet power to the farthest parts of the world, and has a capacity for a battalion of Soviet

marines, some 40 tanks, and other supporting vehicles. It has bow and stern doors, and is capable of accommodating both Air Cushion Vehicles (ACVs) and combat transport helicopters.

The Soviet Navy was starting to assemble an amphibious force of great strategic potential when the Cold War came to an end, and the use to which it will now be put remains to be seen

Above: An overhead view of *Ivan Rogov* illustrating the very large helicopter landing areas and the staggered funnels. This ship can carry a marine battalion, 40 tanks and support vehicles.

Below: Another view of the two landing areas aboard *Ivan Rogov*.

Kresta I and II and Kara Classes

Guided-missile cruisers
20 ships: **Kresta I** — four; **Kresta II** — 10, **Kara** — six.

Kresta I and II classes:
Country of origin: Soviet Union.
Displacement: Kresta I — 6,140 tons (7,500 tons full load); **Kresta II** — 6,000 tons (7,600 tons full load).
Dimensions: Length overall — **Kresta I** — 510ft (155.5m), **Kresta II** — 519.9ft (158.5m); beam (both) 55.7ft (17m); draught (both) 19.7ft (6m).
Aircraft: Kresta I — one Kamov Ka-25 Hormone-B targetting helicopter; **Kresta II** — one Kamov Ka-25 Hormone-A ASW helicopter.
Armament: Kresta I — two twin launchers for four SS-N-3B SSM; 10 21in (533mm) tubes (in two quintets) for Type 53 torpedoes; two twin launchers for SA-N-1 SAM; two twin 2.25in (57mm) guns, four 1.2in (30mm) six-barrelled gatling guns (*Drozd* only); two RBU 6000 12-tubed and two RBU 1000 six-tubed mortars. **Kresta II** — two quad launchers for SS-N-14 SSM; 10 21in (533mm) tubes (in two quintets) for Type 53 torpedoes; two twin launchers for SA-N-3 SAM; two twin 2.25in (57mm) guns, four 1.2in (30mm) six-barrelled gatling guns; two RBU 6000 12-tubed and two RBU 1000 six-tubed mortars.
Propulsion: (both) two steam-turbines (110,000shp); two shafts; four water tube boilers; 35kts.

Kara class:
Country of origin: Soviet Union.
Displacement: 8,000 tons (9,900 tons full load).
Dimensions: Length overall 570ft (173.8m); beam 60ft (18.3m); draught 20ft (6.2m).
Aircraft: one Kamov Ka-25 Hormone-A ASW helicopter.
Armament: Two quad launchers for SS-N-14 SSM; 10 21in (533mm) tubes (in two quintets) for Type 53 torpedoes (two twin tubes in two pairs in *Azov*); two twin launchers for SA-N-3 SAM (one launcher only in *Azov*), six launchers for SA-N-6 SAM (four rounds per launcher, *Azov* only), two twin launchers for SA-N-4 SAM (40 missiles, 10 per launcher); two quad launchers for SS-N-14 ASM; two twin 3in (76mm) guns, four 1.2in (30mm) six-barrelled gatling guns; two RBU 6000 12-tubed and two RBU 1000 six-barrelled mortars (latter not in *Petropavlovsk*).
Propulsion: COGOG. six gas-turbines (four 30,000shp each; two 7,000shp each); two shafts; 34kts.

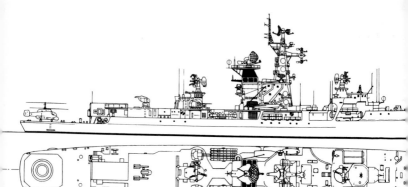

Above: A Kresta II class guided-missile cruiser photographed while it shadowed Western naval forces during a NATO exercise. Shown to advantage are the folding-roofed hangar for the sole Ka-25 Hormone-A ASW helicopter and the extremely small landing platform. The Kresta IIs have a maximum speed of 35kts.

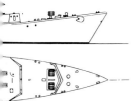

Left: The Kresta II class is an enlarged version of the Kynda class, with a very powerful anti-aircraft and anti-submarine armament. The Kresta I was the initial Soviet ship class to feature a permanent set of facilities to enable helicopter operations, which are vital for target location and SS-N-3 mid-course guidance.

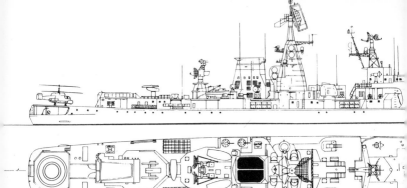

Above: The outline of a Kara class guided-missile cruiser. These are enlarged versions of the Kresta II class and sport improved weapons and electronics fits, as well as gas-turbine engines. Of note is the large mast and very large, separate funnel.

The Soviet guided missile cruisers were originally built in response to the threat posed to the Soviet Union by the large US Navy carrier force. The four Kynda class were the first Russian cruisers to be designed for this purpose. Built between 1960 and 1965, with a standard displacement of 4,800 tons, they were armed with two quadruple-launchers for SS-N-3 SSMs. The large cruise missile has a range of about 475 miles (764km) and is also mounted in the early Soviet cruise-missile armed submarines. The Kyndas have a SA-N-1 SAM twin-launcher forward and two twin 3in (76mm) mounts aft. Two tracking radars are fitted for the SSMs, enabling them to engage two targets simultaneously, but no helicopter is carried. This makes the Kyndas dependent on other ships or aircraft for mid-course guidance for the SSMs. The Kresta Is are enlarged developments of the Kyndas. Whereas the latter design gave priority to the SSM armament, the Kresta Is (and the Kresta II and Kara classes developed from them) have a very powerful anti-aircraft and anti-submarine armament.

In the Kresta Is the SS-N-3 are mounted in pairs on either side of the bridge. They are double-ended vessels, with a SA-N-1 SAM twin-launcher fore and aft on deckhouse magazines. Whereas the Kyndas have two prominent masts and funnels, the Kresta Is have their SSM guidance radar on a single enormous mast amidships. Instead of the Kyndas' long quarterdeck, the Kresta Is have a very short one with a helicopter pad and hangar mounted on it. The Kamov Ka-25 Hormone was designed for anti-submarine work, but could also be used for mid-course guidance for the SSMs. By the late-1960s the ASW problem apparently took precedence and the Kresta IIs were fitted with two quadruple launchers for the long-range SS-N-14 ASW weapon. The SA-N-1 SAMs are replaced by the improved longer-ranged SA-N-3 SAMs. Close-in anti-aircraft defence is provided by the 1.2in (30mm) mounts amidships. Bow sonar is fitted, and as with all modern Soviet warships, a powerful anti-submarine armament is fitted. The helicopter pad and hangar are raised by one deck, which makes them less likely to be damaged in rough seas, and this and the large *Topsail* 3-dimensional radar serve to distinguish the Kresta IIs from the Kresta Is. The Karas are enlarged gas-turbine powered versions of the Kresta IIs. The extra size has been used to mount two retractable SA-N-4 SAM twin launchers, and the heavy anti-aircraft armament has been increased in calibre. They are the first large warships to have gas-turbines, which have been in service with the Soviet Navy in the Kashin class destroyers for over a decade. The Karas can be distinguished from the Kresta IIs by their longer hull and the large separate funnel necessitated by the use of gas turbines. Compared with contemporary American cruisers, the Soviet ships are much more heavily-armed, but the long-range American ships have large and very seaworthy hulls.

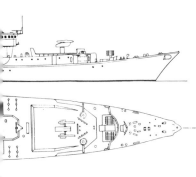

Below: The antennae complexes aboard the Kara class cruiser *Ochakov* are clearly shown. The two identical arrays above the bridge and abaft the funnel are *Headlight* groups, which control the SA-N-4 SAM missiles. At the rear of the bridge is the *Head Net C* air surveillance radar, capable of search and height-finding. Atop the mast is the *Topsail* three-dimensional radar antenna, used for both long-range air surveillance and designation of a variety of potential targets.

Below: A Kara class cruiser caught on film in the Mediterranean Sea. The two quadruple launch silos for the SS-N-14 SSMs are prominent on either side of the bridge. Each missile carries a 1,100lb (500kg) warhead and has a range of 19nm (35km).

Kiev and Modified Kiev Classes

Aircraft carriers
Four ships: **Kiev class** — three; **Modified Kiev class** — one.

Country of origin: Soviet Union.
Displacement: Kiev class — 43,000 tons; **Modified Kiev class** 45,000 tons.
Dimensions: Length 895.7ft (273m); beam 173.9ft (53m); draught **Kiev class** — 31.2ft (9.5m), **Modified Kiev class** — 32.8ft (10m).
Aircraft: 12 Yakovlev Yak-38 Forger-A, one Yak-38 Forger-B fighters; 19 Kamov Ka-27 Helix-A ASW, three Ka-25 Hormone-B targetting helicopters.
Armament: Kiev class — Eight launchers (four pairs) for SS-N-12 SSM; 10 21in (533mm) tubes for Type 53 torpedoes; four launchers (two pairs) for SA-N-3B SAM (10 missiles per launcher), four launchers (two pairs) for SA-N-4 SAM (18 missiles per launcher, *Kiev* and *Minsk* only), four sextuple vertical launchers for SA-N-9 SAM (24 missiles per launcher, *Novorossiysk* only); twin launcher for SUW-N-1 ASM; four 3in (76mm) guns (two pairs), eight 1.2in (30mm) six-barrelled gatling guns; two RBU 6000 12-tubed mortars; **Modified Kiev class** — 12 launchers (six pairs) for SS-N-12 SSM (24 reloads); four sextuple vertical launchers for SA-N-9 SAM (six magazines and 48 missiles per laucher); two 3.9in (100mm) guns, eight 1.2in (30mm) six-barrelled gatling guns; two RBU 12000 10-barrelled mortars.
Propulsion: Four sets of geared turbines (200,000shp); four shafts; 32kts.

During and after the Second World War a formidable Soviet naval air force was built up, consisting of some 4,000 fighters, bombers and reconnaissance planes. In the Khruschev reorganization this was drastically cut back and its fighters removed, but at no time was there any move back to planning aircraft-carriers. In fact the arguments for and against such ships were conducted with

Below: The excellent lines and heavy armament of the Kiev class illustrate the skill and ingenuity of Soviet naval designers. It is clear from the plan view just how the deck has been divided into flight-deck, superstructure and weapons area sections.

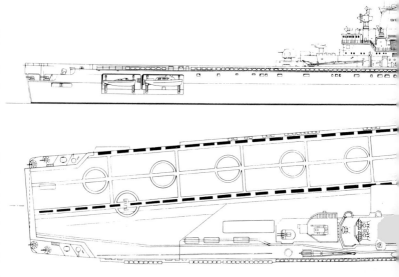

Above: *Kiev* at sea off the United Kingdom during her first cruise.

considerable heat and vigour. The first Kresta I cruiser, comissioned in early 1967, carried a helicopter with a hangar and paved the way for the appearance a year later of *Moskva*, an 18,000-ton helicopter-carrier with 18 Ka-25 Hormone helicopters embarked. She and her sistership *Leningrad* may well have been planned as the forerunners of a large class but no more were completed. Their duties were clearly anti-submarine as reflected in the majority of Soviet type designations for their major ships. They did, however, have considerable potential in other directions such as intervention situations. Shortly before *Moskva* commissioned the first Soviet V/STOL aircraft appeared at an air display near Moscow. Subsequently little else was seen of this type of aircraft and when a large hull was seen building at Nikolayev in 1971 it was no great strain on the intelligence to marry up the two.

The first British Harrier had flown in 1966 and in the next five years had carried out a series of deck-landings on the ships of several navies. When *Kiev* finally

Overleaf: Lined up on the flight-deck of *Kiev* are four Kamov Ka-25 Hormone-B missile-targetting helicopters. Visible in the aircraft parking area is a single Yak-38 Forger-A V/STOL fighter.

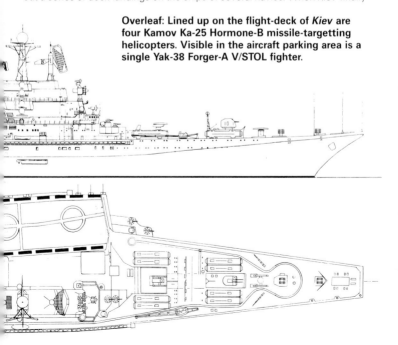

Above: A fine study of *Novorossiysk,* the third and final example of what the Soviet Navy officially refers to as its *takticheskoye avianosny kreyser* — tactical aircraft-carrying cruiser.

Right: Flanking *Minsk's* 3in (76mm) twin-barrelled foredeck gun and (behind it) one of the SA-N-3B twin launchers are four pairs of SS-N-12 SSM launch tubes. Sixteen reloads are carried.

emerged from the Black Sea in August 1976 something totally new was revealed. Not only was she an aircraft-carrier in all but name, she was also a very heavily-armed warship.

Eight anti-ship missile launchers are on her foredeck, with numerous other missiles on the superstructure and 3in (76mm) guns for more conventional defence. She also carries radars and sonar — a major departure from US practice. The first-generation Yak-38 Forger aircraft took some time to work up properly but by the late-1980s were a professional force and displaying a rolling take-off capability which had hitherto been thought impossible in the West. The first two ships, *Kiev* and *Minsk*, are identical, but the third-of-class, *Novorssiysk*, introduced a number of minor changes. The fourth carrier, *Admiral Gorshkov* (originally *Tbilisi*) has so many changes that she is regarded as a separate class on her own. The large *Sky Watch* planar, phased-array radar array mounted on the superstructure, and the *Cake Stand* cylindrical array atop before the stack are among the most obvious visual changes. There are differences in armament as noted in the specifications on page 76, and various steps have been taken to improve the airflow over the flight-deck.

Kilo Class

Patrol submarines
17 boats; five building.

Country of origin: Soviet Union.
Displacement: 2,500 tons surfaced (3,000 tons submerged).
Dimensions: Length overall 239.5ft (73m); beam 31.2ft (9.5m); depth 19.7ft (6m).
Armament: Six 21in (533mm) tubes for 18 Type 53 torpedoes; mines.
Propulsion: Two diesel generators; one electric motor (6,000hp); one shaft; 11kts surfaced (17kts submerged).

Together with France and the United States, Russia was amongst the first countries to appreciate and develop the submarine. The early examples were often crude, but by 1904 more efficient examples had appeared. At the time, Russia was at war with Japan, but the new submarines arrived too late to have any bearing upon the outcome of the conflict.

After the October Revolution of 1917, submarines were developed and acquired to form the backbone of the Soviet naval programme. This continued until the summer of 1941, when over 200 boats were in service. With the conclusion of the Second World War, German technology and expertise became available to the Soviet Union, and plans were drawn up in the immediate post-war years to build 1,200 submarines at the rate of 75 to 100 per year.

In time, the figure of 1,200 boats was scaled down, though those in service still posed a potentially serious threat to the West. The Kilo class made its debut in the late-1970s, with an initial production rate of one boat per year for the Soviet Navy. Subsequent orders from client states (Poland, Romania, India and Algeria) have led to an increase in this production rate. To date, 12 Kilo class boats have been exported, and production continues in Gorky, St. Petersburg and Komsomolsk at a rate of four boats per year. More boats will likely be exported as further elderly Whiskey and Foxtrot class boats are retired from service.

The Kilos feature an improved hull form compared to those of the Foxtrot or Tango classes. However, when compared to the standards of Western submarine design and technology, the Kilos are still somewhat crude. Improving and enhancing operational capabilities is an on-going theme, and at least one boat is believed to feature a surface-to-air missile launcher (most likely for the firing of SA-N-8s) fitted to its fin for a continuing series of firing tests. All boats in the class are coated with *Cluster Guard* anechoic tiles and all have the ability to lay mines via their torpedo tubes.

Above: Initial production of the Kilo class during the late-1970s and early-1980s was one boat per year, but its popularity with overseas customers has boosted this to some four boats per year.

Though somewhat modest when compared to other Soviet submarine designs, the Kilos are still effective patrol submarines. This fact is particularly well appreciated by the Indian Navy, which has eight such boats on strength. Nevertheless, the rapid advances in submarine techology and design will soon render the Kilo class out-of-date.

Below: Though its design and finish lag behind the best in the West, the Kilos remain an effective asset for the Soviet Navy.

Kirov Class

Nuclear-powered battlecruisers
Three ships.

Country of origin: Soviet Union.
Displacement: 28,000 tons full load.
Dimensions: Length overal 813.6ft (248.0m); beam 91.9ft (28.0m); draught 28.9ft (8.8m).
Aircraft: One Kamov Ka-25 Hormone-B targetting and two Kamov Ka-27 Helix-A ASW helicopters.
Armament: 20 SS-N-19 SSM launchers; twin SS-N-14 SSM launcher for 14 missiles (*Kirov*); 12 SA-N-6 SAM VLS for 96 missiles; two SA-N-9 SAM octuple launchers for 128 missiles (*Kalinin* and *Frunze*); two SA-N-4 SAM twin launchers for 40 missiles; six CADS-N-1, each with one 1.12in (30mm) gatling and eight SA-N-11 SAMs (*Kalinin*); 10 21in (533mm) tubes for Type 53 torpedoes (*Kirov* and *Frunze*); two 3.9in (100mm) guns (*Kirov*); two 5in 6130mm) guns (*Kalinin* and *Frunze*); eight 1.12in (30mm) guns (*Kirov* and *Frunze*; *Kalinin* has 12); one RBU 12000 mortar (*Kalinin*); one RBU 6000 mortar (*Kirov* and *Frunze*); one RBU 1000 mortar.
Propulsion: Two nuclear reactors, two oil-fired boilers (150,000shp); two shafts; 32kts.
(Specifications are for *Kalinin; Kirov* and *Frunze* differ in detail.)

Aircraft carriers apart, the largest surface warship to have been designed and built since World War Two was the 17,525 ton displacement, nuclear-propelled cruiser USS *Long Beach* (CGN 9), which was commissioned in 1961. The general impression at the time was that the day of the "big ship" was over and most navies had scrapped their battleships in the 1950s. The sole exception was the US Navy, which had retained four Iowa c ass battleships in reserve (q.v.). It caused very great surprise in naval circles, therefore, when the Soviet Navy constructed a very large new warship, the *Kirov*, which was launched in 1977 and commissioned in 1980.

In terms of dimensions, the Kirovs are only slightly smaller than the Iowas, although they displace rather less (28,000 tons versus 57,500 tons) as they do not have the armoured protection of the American battleships; nor do they have the massive triple 16in (406mm) turrets, each of which weighs some 1,700 tons.

Below: Known to the Soviet Navy as *Raketnyy Kreyser* (missile cruisers), the three Kirov class ships are highly impressive vessels.

Above: All three ships in the Kirov class are able to carry two Ka-27 Helix-A and one Ka-25 Hormone-B helicopters on deck.

They are very elegant ships, with a high freeboard, and are powered by a novel Combined Nuclear and Steam (CONAS) plant. This consists of two nuclear reactors driving two steam-turbines, and two oil-fired boilers driving two quite separate turbines. The exhaust uptakes run through a large mack (combined mast and stack), which is topped by a huge *Top Pair* 3-D air surveillance radar antenna.

Three ships have been commissioned: *Kirov* — 1980; *Frunze* — 1984; and *Kalinin* — 1988. A fourth, *Yuri Andropov*, will join the fleet in 1992. All these ships are exceptionally well armed, but *Frunze* and *Kalinin* have both shown differences from *Kirov*, and, indeed, from each other, and so it can be assumed that the fourth ship will be different again. All the current ships are armed with 20 SS-N-19 anti-ship missile launchers, which are mounted in four rows of five under the foredeck, at an angle of about 40deg. This missile, which is also fitted in Oscar class submarines, is armed with either a conventional or a nuclear warhead, and has a range of some 300nm (570km) at a speed of Mach 2.5. All the ships are also fitted with 12 SA-N-6 vertical SAM launchers and two SA-N-4 medium-range systems, but *Kalinin* has, in addition, six SA-N-11 point-defence systems and has the fittings for the SA-N-9, although this has not yet been installed. *Kirov* mounts two 3.9in (100mm) guns aft, but the later ships have a single twin mount of the new fully automatic, water-cooled 5in (130mm) guns. All have a number of the widely-used 1.12in (30mm) gatling CIWS.

There are also differences in the ASW armament. Both the first two ships have 10 21in (533mm) torpedo tubes, but, interestingly, *Kalinin* does not. The SS-N-14 ASW missile launcher was fitted in *Kirov*, but then discontinued; first deployed in 1974, it is presumably now considered to be obsolete.

Krivak I-III Classes

ASW frigates
Krivak I — 21 ships; **Krivak II** — 11 ships; **Krivak III** — eight ships.

Country of origin: Soviet Union.
Displacement: 3,900 tons full load.
Dimensions: Length overall 410.1ft (125.0m); beam 46.3ft (14.1m); draught 16.1ft (4.9m).
Aircraft: One Kamov Ka-27 Helix-A ASW helicopter.
Armament: One SA-N-4 SAM system; one 3.9in (100mm) automatic DP; two 1.12in (30mm) gatling CIWS; two RBU 6000 ASW RL; eight 21in (533mm) torpedo tubes.
Propulsion: COGOG; two cruise gas-turbines (24,200shp); two high-speed gas-turbines (48,600shp); two shafts; 30kts.

The Krivak class was first seen by Western observers in 1970. It was designed for, among other things, ease of construction and this has enabled it to be built by smaller yards on the Baltic and Black Seas, leaving the larger yards free to concentrate on larger and more complicated warships. To date, it has been built in three versions.

Below: To permit the operation of an ASW helicopter, the two after end 3.9in (100mm) guns have been replaced by a helipad and hangar.

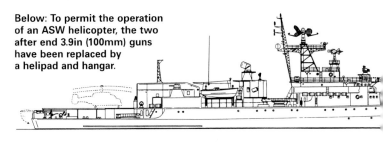

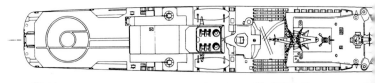

The primary mission of the Krivak Is and IIs is ASW and their primary weapon system is the SS-N-14, a torpedo-carrying missile similar in concept to the US Asroc and Australian Ikara. Four of these missiles are mounted in a large quadruple launcher on the foredeck. This is backed up by two 12-tube RBU 6000 ASW rocket launchers and by two quadruple 21in (533mm) torpedo tubes. Mine-rails are also fitted to both types. The Krivak Is have two twin 3in (76mm) gun turrets mounted aft and in the Krivak IIs, which appeared in 1975, these have been replaced by two single 3.9in (100mm) mounts. The Krivak IIs also incorporate some other, relatively minor, changes, including a larger VDS.

The first Krivak III was seen in 1984 and this version was built specifically for border patrol tasks, with the ships being operated by naval crews, but under the control of the KGB Maritime Border Guard. In this version one 3.9in (100mm) turret is installed forward, leaving the entire after end to be fitted with an ample flight-deck and hangar for a Kamov Ka-27 Helix-A ASW helicopter.

Since its first appearance the long, sleek lines, and combination of powerful armament and effective propulsion system have made the Krivak class an admired sight on the world's oceans. The one disadvantage of the Krivak I and II is that they lack a helicopter facility, and although this has been resolved in the Krivak III this version is not fitted for ASW tasks. It is noticeable that the Soviet Navy has increasingly used these handy frigates as general-purpose destroyers, just as has happened to the US Navy's Oliver Hazard Perry class (q.v.).

A new class of frigate for the Soviet Navy first put to sea in 1991. Designated by NATO Balcom-8 (BALtic COMbattant-8) the first-of-class is now known to be named *Neustrashimy*. These 3,800-ton displacement frigates are the replacements for the elderly Kashin class destroyers and possibly also for the ageing Krivak Is.

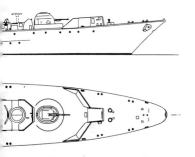

Below: This view of one of 11 Krivak II frigates in service with the Soviet Navy reveals several interesting design features. Dominating the foredeck is a quartet of SS-N-14 launchers, while on the starboard side amidships can be seen four of eight 21in (533mm) torpedo tubes (the other four are on the port side). On the after deck can be seen the stepped pair of 3.9in (100mm) guns, each with a single barrel.

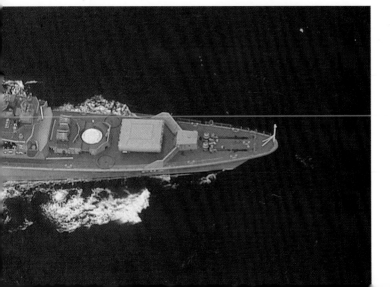

Kuznetsov Class

Aircraft carriers
Two ships.

Country of origin: Soviet Union.
Displacement: 67,500 tons full load.
Dimensions: Length overall 999ft (304.5m); flight deck length 999ft (304.5m); beam 229.7ft (70.37m); draught 34.4ft (10.5m); width 229.7ft (70m).
Aircraft: 12 Su-27B2 Flanker; 12 MIG-29 Fulcrum or 12 Su-25 Frogfoot or 12 Yak-38/41 Forger; 15-18 Ka-27 Helix ASW helicopters.
Armament: 12 SS-N-19 missiles with nuclear capability; four SA-N-9 sextuple launchers (192 missiles); eight SA-N-11 missiles; eight CADS-N-1 twin 1.2in (30mm) gatling guns; numerous smaller guns; two RBU 12000 mortars.
Propulsion: Four steam-turbines; four shafts; 32kts.

The Soviet Navy has always shown a keen interest in aviation. As early as the First World War the naval forces flew a large number of aircraft and by the 1930s the naval air arm was reorganized as part of the fleet programme, with nearly 1,500 aircraft in naval service by 1941. During the Second World War all Soviet naval aircraft flew from land bases with token raids by a few bombers made on Berlin as early as August 1941.

Efforts had been made in the 1930s by the Soviet Union to obtain from the United States plans and components of aircraft carriers. One design, prepared by Cox and Gibbs, was for a hybrid battleships carrier of 72,000 tons and able to operate 30 aircraft using catapults, with a landing deck amidship; but nothing came of the 1,005ft (306.3m) monster. All attempts at acquiring help from any foreign source eventually proved unsuccessful.

By the end of the Second World War, Soviet naval aviation had grown to an impressive size. There were over 1,500 aircraft assigned to the Pacific Fleet alone, but all were still operated from land bases. In spite of the effectiveness of such

a force the Soviets still entertained the ideas of building aircraft carriers, but freely admitted that their construction was beyond their means. However, the abandoned 28,000-ton German aircraft carrier *Graf Zeppelin* had been seized in 1945; she was hastily prepared for sea but sank on her way to the Soviet Union in a violent storm.

The first moves towards Soviet acquisition of a true aircraft carrier came in the 1960s with the emergence of the Moskva class. These vessels bore a resemblance to the Italian *Vittorio Veneto* and French *Jeanne d'Arc* but carried a larger Air Group designed to hunt down enemy SSBNs. They also gave vital experience in the handling of shipborne air operations. Next came the larger Kiev class with their angled deck and the ability to handle an even larger Air Group made up of both fixed-wing aircraft and helicopters. The primary role was again to seek out and destroy enemy SSBNs, but now this could be carried out on a global scale. The *Admiral Kuznetsov* and her sistership *(Varyag)* are a logical step forward from the Kiev class and form the central element of a task force able to operate well away from home base. They are of conventional carrier design, with two starboard side lifts, a 7deg angled deck and a 20deg ski jump.

The hangar is 610ft x 98ft x25ft (185m x 30m x 7.5m) and can house 18 Su-27 aircraft, although up to 60 can be shipped. ASW and reconnaissance is undertaken by Ka-27 Helix helicopters. The SS-N-19 missile launchers are positioned on the forward part of the flight-deck, while the SA-N-9 sextuple vertical launchers are divided into pairs (two midway between the bows and island and two positioned right aft).

The *Admiral Kuznetsov* was laid down in January 1983, launched in early December 1985 and commissioned in January 1991. *Varyag* was laid down in December 1985, launched in November 1988 and is due for completion in 1992. With these carriers the Soviets now possess the basis of an impressive carrier group which will include the powerful Kirov class (q.v.), and extensive deck-landing trials continue using variants of the Su-27 Flanker, Su-25 Frogfoot and Mig-29 Fulcrum fixed-wing fighters.

Below: Representing a most significant advancement in Soviet carrier development, the *Admiral Kuznetsov* sports a 12deg "ski-jump".

Moskva Class

Helicopter cruisers
Two ships.

Country of origin: Soviet Union.
Displacement: 19,200 tons.
Dimensions: Length 623.4ft (190.0m); beam 111.9ft (34.1m) (flightdeck), 85.3ft (26.0m) (hull); draught 24.9ft (7.6m).
Aircraft: 14 Kamov Ka-25 Hormone-A/B/C helicopters.
Armament: Two SA-N-3 SAM launchers; twin SUW-N-1 ASW missile launcher; four 2.25in (57mm) AK-257 DP guns; two RBU 6000 ASW RL.
Propulsion: Two sets geared turbines (100,000shp); two shafts; 30kts.

Moskva entered service in 1967, followed in 1968 by *Leningrad*. They were designed for service mainly in the Mediterranean Sea, with the specific war-time mission of hunting US Navy SSBNs.

The large flight-deck is served by two elevators from the hangar below; there is also a small hangar beneath the massive mack (combined mast and stack). Normally, 14 Ka-25 Hormone ASW helicopters are operated, and although *Moskva* was used for sea trials of the V/STOL Forger, these fighters have never been embarked operationally. Mil Mi-14 Haze-B mine countermeasure helicopters have been embarked on occasion, but are too large for the elevators and must remain on the flight-deck.

The foredeck is entirely devoted to weapons, predominantly for ASW. Two RBU 6000 ASW rocket launchers are mounted in the bows, with an SUW-N-1 ASW twin launcher immediately behind. There are two SA-N-3 SAM launchers, while the two twin 2.25in (57mm) DP guns are mounted either side of the bridge.

Right: The distinctive lines of one of only two Moskva class anti-submarine ships built.

Below right: *Moskva* reveals the profusion of radar antennae on her superstructure, as well as two Ka-25 Hormones on the aft flight-deck.

Below: The size of the flight-deck is shown to good effect in this view. The foredeck is dominated by two SA-N-3 missile launch units.

Above: An RAF Nimrod maritime patrol aircraft takes a close look at the helicopter cruiser *Moskva*.

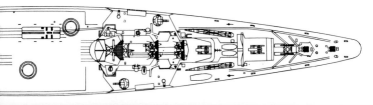

Oscar I-II Classes

Nuclear-powered guided-missile submarines
Oscar I — two boats; **Oscar II** — seven boats (five building).

Country of origin: Soviet Union.
Displacement: 16,000 tons submerged.
Dimensions: Length overall 505.2ft (154.0m); beam 59.1ft (18.0m); draught 32.8ft (10.0m).
Armament: 24 SS-N-19 SSM launchers; six 21in (533mm) and 25.6in (650mm) torpedo tubes for 24 SS-N-15/-16 missiles or torpedoes.
Propulsion: Nuclear. Two pressurized water reactors; two shafts; 33kts. (Specifications are for **Oscar II**).

These huge submarines were designed and built at the same time as the even larger Typhoon class SSBNs, and reflect a recurring Soviet fascination with sheer size. Construction of the first boat started in 1978 and it was launched in 1980, starting trials later that year. It was followed by a second, identical boat two years later; but then production switched to a lengthened hull, whereupon the first two were designated by NATO Oscar I and the new type, Oscar II. As of late-1991 both Oscar Is and seven Oscar IIs were in service, with five more of the latter building.

The Oscar class is the latest in a line of cruise-missile submarines stretching back to the nuclear-powered Echo and diesel-electric Juliet classes of the 1960s. The mission for which they were built was to attack advancing NATO, and in particular US, battle fleets. In the Oscar class the cruise-missile is the SS-N-19, 24 of which are carried in two rows of 12, with missiles bins in pairs covered by a single external hatch. These launch bins are angled upwards at about 40deg

and the missiles, which are of the same type as those installed on the Kirov class battlecruisers (q.v.), are launched while the submarine is submerged. Targeting information is provided from a satellite, which passes information direct to the Oscar via its *Punch Bowl* down-link antenna, although the submarine would have to be very near the surface to receive such EHF signals. The liquid-fuelled SS-N-19 has a range of some 300nm (570km) and a speed of about Mach 2.5.

These submarines have an inner pressure hull some 28ft (8.53m) in diameter and of conventional shape, with the missile bins abreast the small and well-streamlined sail. The outer hull is of elliptical cross-section, which would provide exceptional resistance to most torpedo warheads, and is coated with anechoic tiles designed to reduce the submarine's sonar signature. A large hatch immediately abaft the sail houses a towed VLF communications buoy and a tube atop the vertical stabilizer, fitted on all except the first Oscar I, deploys a towed, linear passive hydrophone array.

The original Oscar I class boats were 469.2ft (143m) in length and the Oscar II is 36.1ft (11m) longer (which results in an increase in displacement of some 1,400 tons), but otherwise they are externally identical. It would appear that either there was some shortcoming in the first boat revealed during its trials (although both Oscar Is have remained in service) or that some additional internal equipment has been installed.

Two former Yankee class SSBNs have been converted to carry SS-N-21 cruise-missiles, thus becoming SSGNs and earning the NATO designation Yankee Notch. However, the SS-N-21 SLCM is a long-range, strategic missile and the mission of the Yankee Notch is thus quite different from that of the Oscar class and other Soviet SSGNs.

Below: One of the two Oscar Is heads for home at slow speed. Noticeable in this view is a somewhat rough exterior — an appearance resulting from the loss at sea of a significant number of its noise-reducing anechoic tiles.

Slava Class

Cruisers
Four ships.

Country of origin: Soviet Union.
Displacement: 9,800 tons standard (11,200 full load).
Dimensions: Length overall 610.2ft (186m); beam 68.2ft (20.8m); draught 24.9ft (7.6m).
Armament: Eight twin launchers for 16 SS-N-12 SSMs; eight launchers for 64 SA-N-6 SAMs (eight rounds per launcher); two twin launchers for SA-N-4 SAMs; 10 21in (533mm) tubes (in two quintets) for Type 53 torpedoes; two 5.1in (130mm) AA guns; six 1.2in (30mm) AA guns (six barrels per mounting); two 12-tube RBU 6000 mortars.
Aircraft: One Kamov Ka-25 Hormone-B targetting helicopter.
Propulsion: Four gas-turbines (120,000hp); two shafts; 34kts.

Built as a follow-on to the Kara and Kresta classes, the four ships constituting the Slava class are a smaller version of the dual-purpose Kirov class (for which they also act as a conventionally-powered back-up). These are very powerful vessels, with a great deal packed into their 11,000-ton full load displacement. Although the design is fairly standard, there is no doubt that they would be able to cope with more highly-developed opponents in times of conflict, well away from their home bases.

The first-of-class ship (*Slava*) was laid down in 1976, launched in 1979 and commissioned in 1982. Two more vessels (*Marshal Ustinov* and *Chervona Ukraina*) have been completed, being commissioned in 1986 and 1990 respectively. The fourth vessel in this class (*Admiral Lobov*) is scheduled to be commissioned during 1993. However, it should be noted that the dwindling resources for defence may well influence future acquisitions for this and other classes. In addition, the growing wave of nationalism may well lead to the renaming of some or all of the Slava class cruisers, in an attempt to diffuse anti-Russian sentiments.

Whatever the future may hold, the fact is that these cruisers are quite formidable weapons platforms. The highly-prominent quartet of twin tubes mounted along

Below: An excellent study of a Slava class cruiser, with the four port-side SS-N-12 SSM angled twin launch tubes clearly visible.

Above: *Marshal Ustinov*, the second-in-class, earns a close look from a US Navy UH-1 helicopter during a US visit in July 1980.

each side of the cruisers' superstructure signal the presence of 16 SS-N-12 SSMs. Each tube has a fixed elevation of 8deg.

Located between the funnels, an additional eight launchers account for the SA-N-6 SAMs, with eight missiles per launcher. However the system is weakened by virtue of having only one radar direction unit. This is mounted vertically in a revolving magazine and uses a track-via-missile guidance system. The missile is multi-purpose and it is claimed that it can intercept a variety of ballistic weapons, as well as low-flying targets with a small radar signature, such as Tomahawk and Harpoon missiles.

A wide range of on-board sensors is backed up by the presence of a single Kamov Ka-25 Hormone-B helicopter, able to provide over-the-horizon targetting data as well as mid-course guidance for launched missiles. Such information can also be provided courtesy of satellite communications.

At present, *Slava* operates as part of the Black Sea Fleet, while *Marshal Ustinov* was deployed to the Northern Fleet on a permanent basis during 1987. The third ship, *Chervona Ukraina*, was assigned to the Pacific Fleet in October 1990.

Sovremenny Class

Guided-missile destroyers
15 ships (seven building).

Country of origin: Soviet Union.
Displacement: 7,850 tons full load.
Dimensions: Length overall 511.8ft (156.0m); beam 57.4ft (17.5m); draught 20.3ft (6.2m).
Aircraft: One Kamov Ka-25 Hormone-B targetting helicopter.
Armament: Eight SS-N-22 SSM launchers; two SA-N-7 SAM systems; two twin 5in (130mm) DP guns; four 21in (533mm) torpedo tubes; two RBU-1000 ASW RL; mines.
Propulsion: Two steam-turbines (100,000shp); 34kts.

These impressive ships were designated BalCom-2 (BALtic Combatant) by NATO until the name of the first-of-class became known. *Sovremenny* (the Russian word for 'modern') was launched in 1978 and has been followed by 14 others since. The class is optimised for surface warfare and the hulls, which are based on those of the Kara II class, have considerably more internal volume than previous classes of Soviet destroyers.

The principle weapons are eight SS-N-22 SSMs, which are mounted in two four-cell bins either side of the bridge. These missiles have a range of some 70nm (133km). There are two twin, fully automatic 5in (130mm) turrets, all of the barrels having water-cooling to achieve a rate of fire of 65rpm per mount. There is a large flightdeck, well forward of the usual position at the stern, with a telescopic hangar which extends aft from the stack.

It is somewhat surprising that this class is powered by conventional steam-turbines rather than by the gas-turbines which successfully power many other classes of Soviet warship. The available evidence suggests that these are pressure-fired, automated steam plants, similar to those fitted in the Kresta class, which were built in the same Zhdanov yard in St Petersburg. However, one of the characteristics of this plant is extremely rapid acceleration (for example, from 10 to 32kts in less than 2 minutes) and it could well be that this is seen to have an advantage in ASW warfare operations.

Construction of the class continues, with the ships already in commission being split equally between the Northern and Pacific Fleets. The class is designated *askadrenny minonosets* by the Soviet Navy, meaning destroyer, although they are, in fact, much more akin to cruisers in both size and capability.

Below: Visible in this view of a Sovremenny class destroyer is the telescopic helipad for a single Ka-25 or Ka-27. Also noticeable is the stern-mounted twin-barrelled 5in (130mm) gun.

Typhoon Class

Nuclear-powered ballistic missile submarines
Six boats.

Country of origin: Soviet Union.
Displacement: 21,500 tons surfaced (26,500 tons submerged).
Dimensions: Length overall 562.7ft (171.5m); beam 75ft (22.8m); depth 40ft (12.2m).
Armament: 20 SS-N-20 ballistic missiles, each with six to nine MIRV warheads of 100kT; two 21in (533mm), four 25.6in (650mm) bow-mounted torpedo tubes; SS-N-15 anti-submarine missiles can be fired from 21in (533mm) tubes, SS-N-16 fired from 25.6in (650mm) tubes; all missiles have nuclear warheads.
Propulsion: Two pressurized water-cooled nuclear reactors; two steam turbines (80,000shp); two shafts; 27kts submerged.

Below: The colossal size of the Typhoon class design can begin to be appreciated when it is realized that the small specks on the bridge are in fact eight members of the boat's crew.

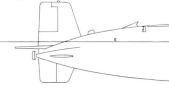

Soviet submarine and surface ship development has made rapid strides over the last 30 years. Every 10 years a clear pattern of fresh concepts have emerged, all of which undergo a periodic degree of refinement. In 1958, the first ballistic missile submarines of the Golf and Hotel classes were introduced. The Yankee class, commissioned in 1967, carried the launch tubes in the hull rather than the fin as in the two previous classes. In 1972 came the first of the Delta class equipped with the new SS-N-8 missile.

The next batch of Deltas had 16 missiles instead of the 12 aboard earlier boats, and were in service in 1976. The Delta III followed soon after, sporting three types of missiles: one with three independently targetted re-entry heads and a range of 2,964nm (5,631km); another of the same range but with seven re-entry vehicles; and a third with a range of 3,641nm (6,919km) but carrying only one warhead.

Below: The Typhoon design uses two parallel pressure hulls as the basis of its construction, each some 29ft 6in to 32ft 10in (9m to 10m) in diameter.

Above: The extremely broad beam of the Typhoon hull can be seen to good effect in this rear view of one of the six boats built.

News of a gigantic submarine under construction at Severodmorsk came in 1977, only 10 years after the introduction of the Yankee SSBNs. At the same time a huge flat hull with numerous holes in its upper surface was reported. There appeared to be no suitable propulsion system for this craft and first reports indicated that it was some form of multi-purpose test-bed able to submerge; but events proved otherwise when in September 1980 the Typhoon class submarine was revealed to the West.

The six submarines in this class are the largest underwater craft in the world and are nearly half as large again as the US's Ohio class. The design differs drastically from that of previous SSBNs, with the 20 missile tubes fitted forward of the large fin which is placed aft of centre. The Anechoic Cluster Guard tile-covered hull houses two separate 28ft (8.5m) diameter compartments placed side-by-side, with a large gap along the sides between the outer and inner hulls. There is a 20ft (6m) diameter pressure-tight compartment in the bow and another under the fin. This configuration gives a fully-integrated weapon system with the two nuclear reactors, one in each hull, being placed alongside the machinery aft of the fin. The rounded hull and squat fin give the Typhoons the ability to force their way through ice up to 10ft (3m) thick. Missiles are SS-N-20 three-stage, solid-fuel SLBMs with stellar inertial navigation guidance and a range of 4,500nm (8,300km). These are able to reach targets anywhere in the world while the submarine remains submerged and in comparative safety.

The Typhoon class can launch two missiles in 15 seconds whilst all the other SSBNs can only deliver one at a time. This unique ability to launch several missiles in a very short space of time at once could also help explain the concentration of the tubes forward of the fin. When several 20-ton missiles are launched together they create a severe trim problem, and by concentrating the tubes aft with the machinery the problem of rapidly-changing trim would be increased.

The huge beam with the ballast tank in the outer casing provides extra protection because of the large "cushion" available should a torpedo strike the outer hull. Only a torpedo that is heavy and able to direct its explosive power well forward could prove adequate, so that its explosive power would not just be absorbed in the surrounding water.

Early tests with the new SS-N-20 missile were not entirely successful, but the problems were eventually ironed out and this weapon now gives the Typhoons a truly formidable capability. The missiles also need little maintenance and with a range of 4,500nm (8,300km) while carrying between six and nine re-entry vehicles, a solitary Typhoon can launch up to 180 missiles in a short period.

The first-of-class boat was laid down in 1977, launched in September 1980 and in service during 1982, with a second unit ready a year later. The programme was completed by 1989, but these large and complex submarines no longer seem to find favour with the Soviets and no more are planned.

Below: The 20 launch tubes arranged in two rows of 10 ahead of the sail each house a single example of the SS-N-20 SLBM.

Principe de Asturias Class

Aircraft carrier
One ship (R 11).

Country of origin: Spain.
Displacement: 16,700 tons full load.
Dimensions: Length overall 642ft (195m); beam 79.7ft (24.3m); draught 30.8ft (9.4m).
Aircraft: Six to 12 McDonnell Douglas AV-8B Harrier II fighters; six to 10 Sikorsky SH-3D/G Sea King, two Sikorsky SH-60B Seahawk and two to four Agusta-Bell AB.212ASW helicopters.
Armament: Four Bazan Meroka 12-barrelled 0.8in (20mm) anti-missile guns; two Rheinmetall 1.45in (37mm) saluting guns.
Propulsion: Two gas-turbines; one shaft; 26kts.

After negotiating considerable financial and technical assistance from the United States, Spain ordered a replacement for the ageing 13,000-ton *Dédalo* in June 1977. The basic design comes from the US Sea Control Ship study of early-1974, but with considerable refinements such as two lifts, one of which is offset to starboard ahead of the island which is placed well aft. The second lift is positioned on the centreline at the after flight-deck edge. A modified flight-deck, which is partly axial, allows for a conventional take-off run by the fixed-wing AV-8B V/STOL aircraft culminating in an integrally structured "ski-jump", so enabling the aircraft to be launched with greater loads. Deck parking is usually on the starboard side aft.

The small island incorporates the command centre and the funnel uptakes. It also houses the only defensive battery of four 12-barrelled Meroka anti-missile guns plus the sea and air radar search and fire control systems.

Laid down at Ferrol in October 1979 and launched in May 1982, *Principe de Asturias* (R 11) was not commissioned until six years later owing to major changes to the command and control systems and the addition of a bridge.

Six to 12 AV-8B Harrier II fixed-wing aircraft plus six to ten SH-3 Sea Kings and up to six SH-60B Seahawk helicopters are carried. The maximum effective operational number of aircraft that can be carried is 24, but by parking on deck up to 37 can be catered for if the need arises. The below deck hangar is nearly 25,000sq ft (2,340m²) in area.

Below: Unlike aircraft carriers in other small navies, Spain's *Principe de Asturias* (R 11) is modern and custom-built for her mission. She is powered by two General Electric gas-turbines.

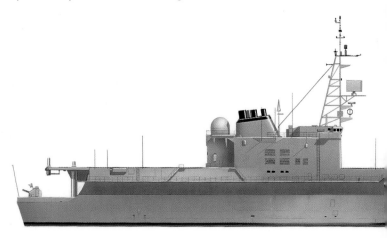

Above: With Italy's *Giuseppe Garibaldi* (C 551) to starboard, *Principe de Asurias* (R 11) cruises in the Mediterranean Sea.

Below: Between six to 12 McDD AV-8B Harrier II V/STOL fighters are embarked aboard the Spanish Navy's aircraft carrier when at sea.

Above: A plan-view before the installation of the "ski-jump".

Västergötland (A 17) Class

Patrol submarines
Four boats.

Country of origin: Sweden.
Displacement: 1,070 tons surfaced (1,143 tons submerged).
Dimensions: Length overall 159.1ft (48.5m); beam 20ft (6.1m); depth 18.4ft (5.6m).
Armament: Six 21in (533mm) tubes, three 15.75in (400mm) tubes; 12 FFV Type 613 torpedoes, six FFV Type 431 torpedoes; 22 mines (fitted externally).
Propulsion: Two Hedemora diesels, one electric motor (1,800shp); one shaft; 11kts surfaced (20kts submerged).

Since World War 2, the Royal Swedish Navy has equipped itself with successive classes of small but very effective submarines built at the Royal Swedish Dockyard at Karlskrona and the Kockums yard at Malmo. The Draken class of 1961-62 were the last to have the traditional hull form, but with the *Sjoormen*, launched in 1967, the modern form was introduced with its short, fat, circular hull without a deck casing. This group of five boats was followed by the three Näcken class boats and the slightly improved Västergötland class, the latter being acquired to replace the outdated Drakens.

Design contracts for the Västergötland class were awarded to Kockums in April 1978, with work commencing in December 1981. Kockums built the midship section and completed final assembly whilst Karlskrona built the bow and stern sections. These boats are single-hulled with an X-type rudder/hydroplane configuration. The Swedish Navy were the first to introduce this form of horizontal and vertical planes and soon began to appreciate its qualities of fine control. Furthermore, it allowed "bottoming" without damage in the shallow Baltic waters. Like the previous designs much thought has gone into achieving economy of space and these compact submarines are ideally suited for service in the relatively small Baltic Sea.

Above: A complement of 21 submariners crew each of the four Västergötland class boats commissioned by the Swedish Navy.

Below: *Hälsingland*, the second-of-class boat, photographed in the Baltic Sea prior to submerging. Torpedoes and mines constitute the boats' weapons, SSMs having been rejected.

Broadsword (Type 22) Class

General-purpose frigates
16 ships: **United Kingdom** — 14 (**Batch 1** — four (F 88-F 91); **Batch 2** — six (F 92-F 96, F 98); **Batch 3** — four (F 85-F 87, F 99)); **Argentina** — two (D 1-D 2).

Country of origin: United Kingdom.
Displacement: Batch 1 — 4,400 tons; **Batches 2/3** — 4,850 tons.
Dimensions: Length (**Batch 1**) — 430.4ft (131.2m); **Batches 2/3** — 485.9ft (148.1m). Beam (all) 48.69ft (14.8m). Draught (**Batches 1/2**) 14.1ft (4.3m), **Batch 3** — 17.7ft (5.4m).
Aircraft: Batch 1 — one Westland Lynx; **Batch 2** — one/two Westland Lynx HAS.3; **Batch 3** — two Westland Lynx or one Westland Sea King.
Armament: Batches 1/2 — four MM38 Exocet SSM; two Sea Wolf GWS.25 SAM; two 1.6in (40mm) Mk 9 AA; six 12.7in (324mm) ASW torpedo tubes; **Batch 3** — eight Harpoon SSM launchers; two Sea Wolf GWS.25 Mod 3 SAM systems; one 4.5in (114mm) Vickers Mk 8 DP gun; one 1.12in (30mm) Goalkeeper CIWS; two 1.12 (30mm) DS-30B AA; six 12.7in (324mm) STWS.2 ASW torpedo tubes.
Propulsion: Batch 1 plus first two of **Batch 2** — COGOG. Two Olympus TM38 gas-turbines (27,300shp each); two Tyne RM1A gas-turbines, (4,100shp); two shafts; 29kts; **Batch 2** (last four) and **Batch 3** — COGAG. Two Rolls-Royce Spey SM.1A DR gas-turbines, (18,770shp each); two Rolls-Royce Tyne RM.1C gas-turbines (5,340shp each); two shafts; 30kts.

Following its very successful Leander class, the Royal Navy designed a successor, the Type 22 ASW frigate, the class taking its name from the first to be launched (12 May 1975): HMS *Broadsword* (F 88). Displacing 4,400 tons, it was planned to build 26 of these ships, which were armed with Sea Wolf SAMs, MM38 Exocet SSMs and ASW torpedo tubes, but lacking any form of gun. Their principle ASW system was the Lynx helicopter. HMS *Broadsword* entered service in 1979, by which time it had already been decided to modify the design by lengthening the hull, which was required to improve seaworthiness and endurance, and to provide extra space for additional weapons and sensors. This resulted in the Boxer (or Type 22 Batch 2) class, the first four ships then being redesignated Batch 1. One of the many lessons of the Falklands War was that guns were still necessary, but it was too late to incorporate any in the Batch 2 ships, although most, but not all, now mount two 1.12 (30mm) AA cannon. Six were built, of which HMS *Sheffield* (F 96) and HMS *Coventry* (F 98) were replacements for the Type 42 destroyers lost in the Falklands War.

The Batch 3 ships use the same hull as the Batch 2s, but with the weapons systems rearranged so that a 4.5in (114mm) gun can be mounted on the forecastle. The Exocet SSMs have been replaced by Harpoons, which are mounted abaft the bridge. In addition, a Dutch Goalkeeper CIWS has been mounted immediately before the mast.

The only overseas orders placed for this class were for two Batch 1 ships by the Argentine Navy. The first, *Hercules*, was built in Britain and entered service in 1976, while the second, *Santissima Trinidad*, was built in Argentina.

Below: HMS *Brave* (F 94), the third Batch 2 frigate, was laid down in 1982, launched in 1983, and commissioned in 1986.

Below: HMS *Broadsword* (F 88) underway in the English Channel. Prominent on her foredeck are the four MM 38 Exocet SSM launchers, while the upper deck is headed by a pair of six-barrelled Sea Wolf SAM launchers. Also visible on the port-side amidships is one of the two 1.6in (40mm) Mk 9 AA guns fitted as standard.

108

Duke (Type 23) Class

General-purpose frigates
Four ships (F 229-F 231, F 233); six building (F 234-F 239).

Country of origin: United Kingdom.
Displacement: 4,200 tons full load.
Dimensions: Length overall 436.4ft (133.0m); beam 52.8ft (16.1m); draught
14.1ft (4.3m).
Aircraft: One Westland Lynx or (from mid-1990s) Agusta-Westland EH.101
Merlin ASW helicopter.
Armament: Eight Harpoon SSM launchers; one Seawolf SAM vertical
launch group; one 4.5in (114mm) Mk 8 DP gun; two 1.12in (30mm) DS-30B
AA cannon; four 12.7in (324mm) ASW torpedo tubes.
Propulsion: CODLAG: two Rolls-Royce Spey SMIA gas-turbines; four
Paxman Valenta 12 RPA 200CZ diesel generator sets; two electric motors
(41,250shp); two shafts; 28kts.

The Royal Navy's Duke (Type 23) class frigates were planned as the successor
to the very successful Leander class, 25 of which were built between 1960 and
1973. Design work started in the late-1970s and was progressing well when the
Falklands War took place. A major consequence of the lessons learned from
the naval campaign (where the Royal Navy lost three warships) was that a major redesign became necessary and the ship's size increased considerably to
accommodate the changes. At one stage it was planned to build at least 17,
but the final figure is now uncertain, in view of the British Defence cuts resulting
from the end of the Cold War. Ten were on order in late-1991, of which the first,
HMS *Norfolk*, was commissioned in July 1989 followed by HMS *Marlborough*
in 1990, and HMS *Argyll* and HMS *Lancaster* in 1991, with the remaining seven
scheduled to join the fleet between 1992 and 1995.

The Duke class design is unusual in Royal Navy practice in having a flush-decked hull and a large angular stack, instead of the usual well-rounded design. It also has the first bow sonar to be fitted in a Royal Navy ship, all previous installations having been hull-mounted. There is a large hangar and the flight-deck is fitted, again for the first time in a British warship, with a haul-down system. The current ASW helicopter is the Westland Lynx, but this will be replaced by the Anglo-Italian EH 101 Merlin when it enters service.

The propulsion system is most unusual, being CODLAG — Combined Diesel Electric and Gas-turbine. Each of the electric propulsion motors is built around one of the shafts and can be powered by any combination of the diesel generators. These are used for quiet running, especially when hunting submarines, giving speeds of up to 15kts. For higher speeds the gas-turbines are switched in. The propellers are fixed-pitch and astern drive can only be obtained using the two electric motors.

Main armament is concentrated on the foredeck. There is a single Vickers 4.5in (114mm) DP gun, behind which is a deckhouse/magazine containing the vertical launch tubes for the Sea Wolf SAM system, which has proved its effectiveness in both the Falklands and Gulf Wars. Between this and the bridge are the eight Harpoon SSM tubes, four firing on either beam.

Considerable efforts have been made to reduce the ships' radar signature. All upright surfaces are sloped at 7deg, edges are rounded and infra-red emissions have been reduced as far as is practicable.

A surprising omission is a CIWS gun, such as a Dutch Goalkeeper. However, there is some discussion of lengthening the hull in later ships (as has been done with the later batches of both Types 22 and 42). This would permit an increase in the size of the Sea Wolf VLS and the fitting of at least one Goalkeeper.

Below: Destined to form a major element within the Royal Navy of the 1990s and beyond, the Duke class frigate incorporates much stealth technology to reduce acoustic, magnetic, radar and infra-red signatures. Illustrated is HMS *Norfolk* (F 230).

Invincible Class

Light aircraft carriers
Three ships (R 05-R 07).

Country of origin: United Kingdom.
Displacement: 20,600 tons.
Dimensions: Length 689ft (210m); beam 118.1ft (36m); draught 21.3ft (6.5m).
Aircraft: Nine BAe Sea Harrier FRS.1; three Westland Sea King Mk.2A AEW and nine Westland Sea King HAS.Mk 6 ASW helicopters.
Armament: One Sea Dart GWS.30 Mod 2 SAM system; **HMS *Invincible*** — three 1.12in (30mm) Goalkeeper CIWS; **HMS *Illustrious*** — two 0.8in (20mm) Mk15 CIWS; **HMS *Ark Royal*** — three 0.8in (20mm) Mk15 CIWS; four Sea Wolf GWS.26 Mod 2 lightweight SAM systems (after current refits); two 0.8in (20mm) GAM-B01 AA guns.
Propulsion: Four Rolls-Royce Olympus TM.3B gas-turbines (112,000shp); two shafts; 28kts.

Below: An excellent illustration of HMS *Invincible* (R 05) while on manoeuvres. Visible on deck is a Seak King helicopter and a pair of Sea Harrier fighters. The latter make full use of the "ski-jump".

Following the 1960s political decision to cancel the proposed attack carrier (*CVA-01*), design work started on a new type of large, air-capable, ASW cruiser, intended for deployment into NATO's Eastern Atlantic (EASTLANT) area of operations. The design went through a series of changes in response to both political and naval manoeuvring in the British Ministry of Defence, one facet of which was the somewhat transparent attempt to disguise the ships' purpose by describing them as "through-deck cruisers", rather than as "aircraft carriers". Originally intended only to operate large ASW helicopters, late design changes had to be made to enable them to operate Sea Harrier fighters as well.

The Invincible class has an open forecastle head deck enabling them to mount a twin-arm Sea Dart SAM launcher, supplemented, as a result of experience in the Falklands War, by a CIWS: a Dutch Goalkeeper in the case of HMS *Invincible* and a Mk15 Phalanx in the other two. The other CIWS are mounted in various positions in the three ships. All ships also have a twin 0.8in (20mm) GAM-BO1

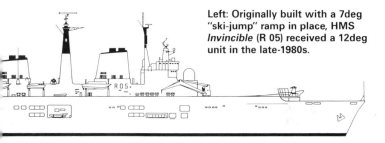

Left: Originally built with a 7deg "ski-jump" ramp in place, HMS *Invincible* (R 05) received a 12deg unit in the late-1980s.

anti-aircraft gun fitting. Four Sea Wolf lightweight SAM launchers are being installed during the current round of refits.

The flight-deck is 550ft (167.8m) long and 44ft (13.4m) wide, and is slightly offset to port to clear the Sea Dart launcher. HMS' *Invincible* (R 05) and *Illustrious* (R 06) were built with a 7deg "ski-jump" and HMS *Ark Royal* (R 07) was the first to have the full 12deg device, which is now being fitted to the other two during refit.

The aircraft complement is a mix of Sea Harrier V/STOL fighters and Sea King helicopters. The initial peacetime complement was five Sea Harriers, but experience shows that nine is the minimum, operationally acceptable number. Originally it was planned to embark only ASW helicopters, but the Falklands War showed that no Carrier Group can operate safely without airborne early warning (AEW) cover and, as a result, three Sea King AEW helicopters are now a standard component of the Air Group. The balance of helicopters — usually nine — are all ASW types.

One of the most important facilities provided by these ships are their command, control and communications (the so-called C³) facilities. They have a very

Above: This elevated view of HMS *Ark Royal* (R 07) reveals the classic deck-to-port, island-to-starboard carrier configuration.

Below: Replenishment-at-sea is vital if aircraft carriers are to perform missions of long duration. Here, HMS *Illustrious* (R 06) takes on fuel from the fleet tanker RFA *Olmeda* (A 124).

sophisticated installation, and are invariably employed as flagships.

These three ships are employed by the Royal Navy on a rotating basis. Two are always in full commission with the fleet, while the third is either being employed as a dockside trainer (and could be reactivated in an emergency) or is in major refit. Thus, HMS *Invincible* was in refit from March to May 1989, at which point HMS *Illustrious* was laid-up for training pending her major refit, which will last from 1991 to 1993; then HMS *Ark Royal* will be laid-up, and so on.

These ships have proved a great success, maintaining the Royal Navy's carrier capability when it had appeared to be doomed. It has to be admitted that their capabilities are limited compared to those of a fully-fledged fleet carrier, but, as was shown by HMS *Invincible* in the Falklands War (accompanied by the conventional carriers HMS *Hermes*), the aircraft they embark can make the difference between success and failure, especially in distant waters.

Below: The more pronounced 12deg "ski-jump" incorporated in HMS *Ark Royal* (R 07) can be seen to good effect in this portrait.

Resolution Class

Nuclear-powered ballistic missile submarines
Four boats: S 22-S 23, S 26-S 27.

Country of origin: United Kingdom.
Displacement: 7,500 tons surfaced (8,400 tons submerged).
Dimensions: Length overall 425ft (129.5m); beam 33in (10.1m); draught 30ft (9.1m).
Armament: 16 Lockheed Polaris A3 two-stage SLBMs, each with three 200kT MRV warheads; Chevaline nuclear warheads; six 21in (533mm) tubes for Marconi Tigerfish Mk 24 Mod 2 torpedoes.
Propulsion: One Rolls-Royce pressurized water-cooled reactor; one set English Electric steam-turbines; 25kts submerged.

In the late-1950s it had been planned that the Royal Air Force would provide the British strategic deterrent in the 1960s and 1970s using 'V' bombers armed with Skybolt, a stand-off missile then under development in the USA. However, at the Nassau Conference in 1962 President Kennedy told Britain that America was unilaterally abandoning the Skybolt project because of development difficulties. It was decided at that conference that Britain should build her own nuclear ballistic missile submarines. The Polaris SLBMs would be provided by the US, but Britain would fit her own warheads.

Four submarines were commenced, and when *Resolution* (S 22) was laid down in February 1964 it was announced that a fifth Polaris submarine was to be ordered. This would ensure that one would always be available on patrol, but this boat was cancelled in 1965 as part of the Labour government's savage cost-cutting defence review.

The actual design was based on that of the Valiant class SSNs, with a new missile compartment inserted between the control room and the reactor compartment. The missiles were refurbished in the mid-1980s and a new type

Above: The nuclear-powered ballistic missile submarine (SSBN) HMS *Resolution* (S 22) expelling air from her tanks immediately prior to diving. Primary armament is 16 Polaris A3 SLBMs.

of British warhead fitted with elaborate penetration aids and designated Chevaline, were fitted, with each missile now carrying three 200kT MRVs. The Resolution class will be progressively phased out as the new Vanguard class, currently under construction, enters service between 1994 and 1998. However, this schedule is under serious threat as a result of cracks found in the area of the nuclear reactor cooling pumps aboard three of the four Resoltuion class boats. At least two of the boats are currently out of commission due to these technical difficulties.

Below: HMS *Repulse* (S 23) at speed on the surface. The Royal Navy had planned to build five of these SSBNs in order to be able to guarantee a minimum of one boat being on patrol at any one time, which is necessary if a credible deterrence is to be maintained. Unfortunately this was cancelled, production ending at four boats.

Trafalgar Class

Fleet submarines
Seven boats (S 87-S 88, S 90-S 93, S 107).

Country of origin: United Kingdom.
Displacement: 4,700 tons surfaced (5,208 tons submerged).
Dimensions: Length overall 280.1ft (85.4m); beam 32.1ft (9.8m); depth 31.2ft (9.5m).
Armament: Five 21in (533mm) tubes for Tigerfish Mk 24 Mod 2 and Spearfish torpedoes; UGM-84B Sub-Harpoon SSM; ground mines.
Propulsion: One pressurized water-cooled PWR nuclear reactor (4,000hp); one shaft; pump jet propulsion (except **S 107**); 32kts submerged.

The seven boats of the Trafalgar class closely follow the design of the previous Swiftsures, which proved a great success. This latter class had shorter, fatter hulls coupled with a shorter sail which reduced the periscope depth. They also had a coating of the new anechoic tiles for noise reduction which made them

Below: Assigned to the 2nd Submarine Squadron, Royal Navy, HMS _Tireless_ (S 88) is one of seven Trafalgar class boats ordered.

Above: A complement of 97 crew, 12 of whom are officers, man each Trafalgar class boat. Additional boats may yet be built.

Overleaf: HMS *Turbulent* (S 87), seen here surfacing, was the first-of-class boat. Additional boats may yet be built.

the quietest of SSNs. As six years had passed between the two designs it was possible to incorporate the many advances made in detection and electronics, and the Trafalgars incorporate the latest in "quietening" technology. Other improvements include a propulsion plant featuring a new core which has a longer life than previous types.

The increased size of the Trafalgar class boats and the many improvements made to their equipment has greatly increased their individual cost. Back in 1976, HMS *Swiftsure* (the first of her class) cost £37.1 million; the cost for the fifth boat in the class — HMS *Spartan* — rose to £68.9 million. Costs are even higher within the Trafalgar class: HMS *Torbay* (the fourth boat) has now cost £176 million; whilst HMS *Triumph* has cost over £200 million!

In order to achieve even quieter running, the machinery raft is suspended from bulkheads at each end of the engine spaces and not the hull as in the Swiftsure class. A pump jet is employed instead of the conventional propeller, so cutting down even more on noise. Such improvements occasionally present problems (and here it is weight), but the additional buoyancy of the tail cone enables this extra load to be carried. Trials with the pump jet were not completed in time for the system to be used in the first-of-class, HMS *Trafalgar*, and a conventional shaft was fitted; but the pump has been incorporated in subsequent boats. The hulls are covered in anechoic tiles to further reduce the acoustic sound level. These boats also carry a new array of sensors, with the Type 2020 sonar in the bow and a Type 2019 mounted ahead of the fin. Torpedo tubes are fitted as in the Swiftsure boats, with two firing from each side, the four tubes being angled out from abaft the bow sonar. The fifth tube is located on the underside of the hull. Both Tigerfish and Spearfish torpedoes are carried. The Tigerfish wire-guided/acoustic-homing ASW torpedo has an electric motor with twin contra-rotating propellers; speed is approximately 50kts and range is 11nm (21km). Spearfish is also wire-guided, with active/passive homing to 34nm (65km) at 60kts. Also carried is the Sub-Harpoon SSM, a sub-launched version of the US anti-ship missile which has proved highly successful. Urchin and Stonefish ground mines can be carried in place of torpedoes.

HMS *Trafalgar* was ordered in 1977, laid down in 1979 and commissioned in 1983. Five more units (HMS' *Turbulent, Tireless, Torbay Trenchant* and *Talent*) followed from 1984 to 1990, leavng the final boat (HMS *Triumph*) to be completed during 1992. Looking to the future, plans to modernize the fleet will include trials with a revised wet end to the towed sonar, and an upgraded radar.

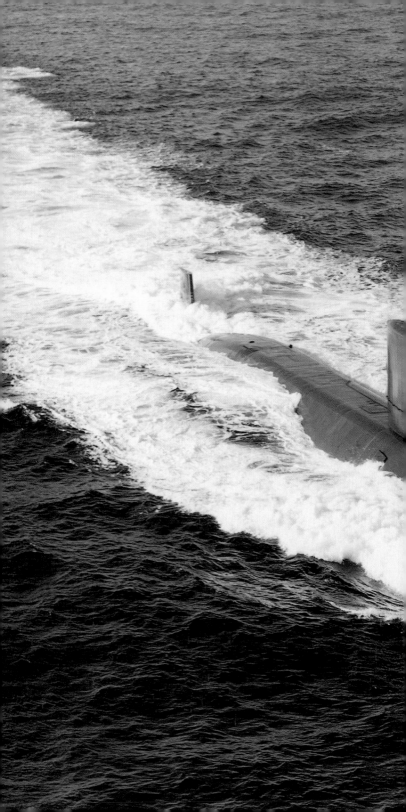

Type 42 Class

Guided-missile destroyers

12 ships: **Batch 1** — four (D 86-D 88, D 108); **Batch 2** — four (D 89-D 92); **Batch 3** — four (D 95-D 98).

Country of origin: United Kingdom.
Displacement: Batches 1/2: 4,250 tons; **Batch 3:** 4,775 tons.
Dimensions: Length: **Batches 1/2:** 410.1ft (125.0m), **Batch 3:** 462.9ft (141.1m); Beam: **Batches 1/2:** 47.1ft (14.34m), **Batch 3:** 48.9ft (14.9m); Draught: **Batches 1/2:** 14.1ft (4.3m), **Batch 3:** 13.8ft (4.2m).
Aircraft: One Westland Lynx HAS.3.
Armament: One Sea Dart GWS.30 SAM system; one 4.5in (114mm) Vickers Mk 8 DP gun; two 0.8in (20mm) Mk 15 gatling CIWS; two 0.8in (20mm) GAM-B01 AA guns; two 0.8in (20mm) Oerlikon AA guns; six 12.7in (324mm) STWS.1 ASW torpedo tubes.
Propulsion: COGOG. Two Rolls-Royce Tyne RM.1C gas-turbines (5,340shp each); two shafts; 28kts (**Batches 1/2**) 29.5kts (**Batch 3**).

The Type 42 destroyers were designed as a cheaper version of the very expensive Type 82, which had been intended as the escorts for the proposed aircraft carrier, CVA-01, and only one of which, HMS *Bristol*, was eventually built. The role of the Type 42 was to act as air defence pickets for task groups centred upon Invincible class carriers, since at that time there was no intention of having AEW helicopters. Known as the Sheffield class, the nameship was commissioned in 1975 and was followed by five more Batch 1 vessels and four more of the very similar Batch 2.

The Batch 3 ships, like the Type 22 Batch 2/3 (pages 106-109), have been lengthened, which was intended to improve seaworthiness, range and accommodation standards. It is noteworthy, however, that all the Type 42 Batch 3 ships have had to have a prominent hull strake and doubler plates fitted, which suggests that the hull had insufficient strength for the additional length. There was no change in armament, but most of the sensors were upgraded. The four ships of this batch were commissioned between 1982 and 1985. All the hulls have an estimated operational life of 22 years.

Below: HMS *Edinburgh* (D 97), the third of four Batch 3 Type 42 class destroyers for the United Kingdom's Royal Navy. This quartet of ships can be distinguished by virtue of their lengthened hull.

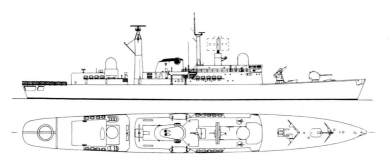

Above: Note the 4.5in (114mm) gun and twin Sea Dart SAM launcher.

Above: The two large domes visible aboard HMS *Birmingham* (D 86) house the Marconi Type 909 or 909 Mod 1 fire control radars.

Upholder Class

Patrol submarines
Four boats (S 40-S 43).

Country of origin: United Kingdom.
Displacement: 2,455 tons submerged.
Dimensions: Length overall 230.6ft (70.3m); beam 25ft (7.6m); depth 7.7ft (5.5m).
Armament: Six 21in (533mm) tubes for Tigerfish Mk 24 Mod 2 and Spearfish torpedoes; UGM-84B Sub-Harpoon SSM; ground mines.
Propulsion: Two Paxman diesels, one electric motor (5,400hp); one shaft; 12kts surfaced (20kts submerged).

By the end of the 1970s, the Royal Navy was in need of a new class of non-nuclear submarine, and in 1979 plans were formulated for the Type 2400, later known as Upholder. The previous diesel-powered class, completed in 1967, had proved successful in service and were much quieter than their nuclear-powered counterparts. Moreover, Vickers (Barrow) were the only remaining shipyard in the UK with nuclear building experience, and they were already committed to the Trident programme, so cutting down on construction capacity.

The first boat (HMS *Upholder*) was laid down at the Vickers Shipbuilding and Engineering Yard at Barrow-in-Furness in November 1983, launched in December 1986 and commissioned in June 1990. Three more boats (HMS' *Unseen, Ursula* and *Unicorn*) are being built by Cammell Laird of Birkenhead, but the last of these will not be completed until 1993. Four more boats were originally planned but cancelled as a cost-cutting exercise and as a way of reducing the Royal Navy's diesel-powered submarine fleet to four boats by 1995.

The hull is single-skinned and made of high-tensile steel, with a "teardrop" shape for maximum underwater efficiency. The hull form has an unusually high beam to length ratio, and the large diameter of the pressure hull enables a spacious two-deck layout to be incorporated. Two watertight bulkheads divide the pressure hull into three main watertight compartments, with an acoustic bulkhead separating the propulsion room aft of the engine room. The overall design is amongst the best available, and like most modern submarines is capable of diving to great depth; in this case over 650ft (200m).

By using high-tensile steel greater strength is given to the hull structure, so

Below: HMS *Upholder* (S 40) was commissioned into service on 9 June 1990. A crew of 47 is carried, of which seven are officers.

enabling an increase of up to 50 per cent in diving depth. A decade ago, the Soviets were still using steel for the majority of submarines; but several classes have since been built of titanium which has greatly increased their diving capability (now estimated to be 2,000ft to 3,000ft (607m to 914m). By using titanium, which is non-magnetic, the hull is virtually undetectable to airbourne MAD and complex sea-laid coils, but welding the hull sections presents great problems. In the early-1970s, the West Germans tried to overcome the detection of their small Type 205, 206 and 207 submarines which usually operated in the shallow Baltic waters by using non-magnetic steel, but without success as corrosion proved too serious a problem.

Main machinery comprises two Paxman Valenta 1600 RPA-200 SZ diesels: the first time these engines have been fitted to submarines. At present, the Upholders carry Marconi Tigerfish Mk 24 Mod 2 torpedoes, but the more sophisticated and faster Spearfish will eventually be available. Both systems can be used either against surface craft or submarines. Endurance is 49 days, and each boat can run at 3kts submerged for 90 hours.

Below: Immediately apparent in this view of HMS *Upholder* is the very high sail, and the prominent sonar dome located on the foredeck.

Below: Wearing the red pennant to indicate sea trials prior to its acceptance into service is HMS *Unseen* (S 41), the second boat in this class of diesel-electric patrol submarines built for the Royal Navy's Submarine Flotilla.

Vanguard Class

Nuclear-powered ballistic missile submarine
One boat (05); two building (06-07); one projected (08).

Country of origin: United Kingdom.
Displacement: 15,000 tons submerged.
Dimensions: Length overall 491.8ft (149.9m); beam 42ft (12.8m); depth 39.4ft (12m).
Armament: 16 vertical tubes (in two rows of eight) for 16 Trident 2 (D5) SLBM; four 21in (533mm) tubes for Tigerfish Mk 24 Mod 2 and Spearfish torpedoes.
Propulsion: One pressurized, water-cooled PWR2 reactor; geared steam turbines; one shaft; 25kts submerged approx.

In July 1980, the British Government announced that it was acquiring from the United States the Trident I weapon system, comprising the C4 ballistic missile with supporting systems, for a new class of British-built submarines to replace the rapidly ageing Polaris force in the early-1990s.

In March of the following year, the Government decided to obtain the improved Trident 2 SLBM armed with the D5 weapon to be carried by four submarines now to be ready by the mid-1990s. The original programme called for one boat per year, but after the first vessel, HMS *Vanguard* (05), was ordered in April 1986, the gaps in ordering became longer, and the final vessel (08 — as yet unnamed) has still not been laid down.

This delay in the programme has added to the already high cost of the programme, much of which is borne by the Royal Navy. This has an added disadvantage of forcing the Navy to postpone the follow-on to the Trafalgar class, as well as weakening the re-equipment programme for the rest of the fleet.

HMS *Vanguard* is scheduled to be commissioned during 1992, with the second boat, HMS *Victorious* (06), in 1994 and the third, HMS *Vigilant* (07), by the following year. All units in this class will be built by Vickers Shipbuilding and Engineering Ltd.

Below: An artist's impression of HMS *Vanguard* (05), the first of four Vanguard class SSBN's planned for the Royal Navy.

Above: Slowly but surely, HMS *Vanguard* takes shape in the Vickers Shipbuilding and Engineering Ltd shipyard in 1992.

Like many present-day submarines, the Vanguard class hull is covered with a conformal anechoic noise-reduction coating. This, combined with the carefully contoured hull, will greatly reduce the boats' underwater noise.

The Vanguards' primary armament comprises 16 Lockheed Trident 2 (D5) SLBMs, powered by three-stage solid-fuel rockets and with on-board stellar guidance up to 6,500nm (12,350km). Although each SLBM can carry up to 12 MIRVs, they will be restricted to a maximum of eight in Royal Navy service, all of which will be manufactured in the UK. Torpedoes will include Marconi's Tiger-fish and Spearfish models.

The main machinery consists of one pressurized water-cooled PWR 2 nuclear reactor; while geared turbines develop 27,500shp, to give a speed of 25kts submerged. Refitting and recoring of the reactor will occur every eight years.

Forrestal Class

Aircraft carriers
Four ships: CV 59-CV 62.

Country of origin: United States.
Displacement: 79,250 tons.
Dimensions: Length 1,086ft (331.0); beam 130ft (39.63m); draught 37ft 1in (11.3m).
Aircraft: 20 Grumman F-14 Tomcat; 20 McDonnell Douglas F/A-18 Hornet; 16 Grumman A-6E Intruder; five Grumman EA-6B Prowler; five Grumman E-2C Hawkeye; eight Lockheed S-3A/B Viking; and six Sikorsky SH-3 Sea King or Sikorsky SH-60F Seahawk ASW helicopters.
Armament: Two Mk 29 launchers for Sea Sparrow SAM; three 0.8in (20mm) Mk 15 CIWS.
Propulsion: Four sets GE geared-turbines (260,000shp); four shafts; 33kts.
(Specifications above are for USS *Forrestal* (CV-59); others differ in detail).

United States (CVA-58), the first post-war American aircraft carrier to be laid down, had a designed displacement of 65,000 tons. She was to have had funnels flush with the flight deck and a retractable bridge to provide the maximum possible deck space for operation of the large post-war carrier aircraft. However, she was cancelled almost immediately after being laid down in April 1949 because of doubts about her design and function, and because of pressure from the USAF Strategic Air Command. The subsequent "Admirals' revolt" and a reassessment of the value of aircraft carriers in the light of the Korean War resulted in the US Navy being allowed to build a fleet based on large aircraft carriers. A Forrestal was authorized each year

Right: USS *Forrestal* (CV-59), 79,250 tons full load, was commissioned in October 1955.

Below: A fine study of USS *Ranger* (CV-61) on patrol in the Indian Ocean. The first carriers specifically built to operate jet aircraft, they remain an important asset to the US Navy.

from 1952-55, and USS' *Forrestal* (CV-59), *Saratoga* (CV-60), *Ranger* (CV-61) and *Independence* (CV-62) were built between 1952-59. They were the largest aicraft carriers to be built since the Japanese *Shinano* of 1944. Their design was based on that of the *United States* (CVA-58), but it was modified to take advantage of the new British angled deck. This underwent very successful trials on the Essex class aircraft carrier *Antietam* (CV-36) in 1952, and gave the necessary deck space whilst still retaining a fixed island and funnel. *Forrestal* (CV-59) was the first American aircraft carrier to be built with an angled deck. This is angled at 8deg and the flight deck and island are sponsored out to twice the width of the hull. The four lifts, each 52ft 3in by 62ft (15.9m by 18.9m) are external to the hull, eliminating a source of weakness in previous carriers' flight decks. *Forrestal* (CV-59) was also the first American carrier to be built with steam catapults (another British invention), having two forward and two on the angled deck enabling four aircraft to be launched in very rapid succession. To improve seaworthiness the Forrestals have a fully-enclosed hurricane bow, the first fitted to an American carrier since the pre-war Lexingtons. However, when first completed they were unable to maintain high speed in rough weather because the forward 5in (127mm) gun sponsons were liable to structural damage because of their size and position. They were therefore removed and later the remaining guns were also deleted, being replaced by three Mk 29 Sea Sparrow launchers. Another weak point in the design is the positioning of the port lift at the forward end of the angled deck where it interferes with flying operations. *Saratoga* (CV-60), *Ranger* (CV-61) and *Independence* (CV-62) are slightly larger than *Forrestal*, and have more powerful engines giving a knot more speed. *Ranger* (CV-61) has a wider flight deck and *Independence* (CV-62) is slightly longer. Since the phasing out of the Essex class carriers, they all now operate a mix of fighter, attack, airborne radar, reconnaissance and ASW aircraft and helicopters.

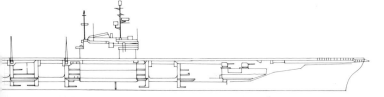

Iowa Class

Battleships
Four ships (BB 61-BB 64).

Country of origin: United States.
Displacement: 57,500 tons full load.
Dimensions: Length overall 887.1ft (270.4m); beam 108.2ft (32.97m);
draught 38.0ft (11.6m).
Aircraft: Four helicopters (no hangar — see text).
Armament: 32 Tomahawk SLCM launchers; 16 Harpoon SSM launchers;
nine Model 1936 16in (406mm) guns; 12 5in (127mm) Mk 12 Mod 1 DP
guns; four 0.8in (20mm) Mk15 gatling CIWS, eight 0.5in (12.7mm) MG.
Propulsion: Four sets geared turbines (212,000shp) four shafts; 33kts.

The US Navy started design work on the Iowa class of fast battleship in 1938,
the first-of-class, USS *Iowa* (BB 61) being laid down on 27 June 1940, launched
on 27 August 1942 and commissioned on 22 February 1943. She was followed
by USS *New Jersey* (BB 62) three months later, and by USS *Missouri* (BB 63)
and USS *Wisconsin* (BB 64) in 1944.

  All four ships fought with great distinction in the Pacific campaign. After the
war, however, there was almost universal agreement that the era of the battleship was over; but, while other navies scrapped their battleships in the 1950s,
the US Navy decided to retain the four battleships in reserve. They were all reactivated for use in the shore bombardment role during the Korean War (1950-53)
and were then "mothballed" once again. USS *New Jersey* was reactivated for
the Vietnam War in 1967, but was decommissioned yet again in 1969.

  The appearance of the Soviet Kirov class battlecruisers (q.v.) caused yet another
reappraisal of these fine but ageing ships. Then, after a lot of discussion it was
decided to reactivate them and give them a limited modernization. USS *New
Jersey* joined the Pacific Fleet on 28 December 1982 and started her first operational deployment on 9 June 1983, returning to the United States on 5 May 1984.
These activities took her to waters off Central America and the Lebanon, one
of the longest peacetime deployments in the history of the US Navy, during which
she covered 76,000nm (144,400km) in 322 days. USS *Iowa* was recommission-
ed in April 1984, USS *Missouri* in 1986 and USS *Wisconsin* in 1988.

  The modernization programme involved updating the electronic equipment,
renovation of living accommodation, conversion to the use of distillate fuel, reshap-
ing the after deck to accommodate four helicopters (although no hangar was
installed), and the removal of all extraneous equipment. The main armament
remained the 16in (406mm) guns, firing 2,700lb (1,225kg) projectiles to a maximum range of 20.6nm (39km). USS *Iowa* suffered a major explosion, thought
to have been deliberate, in one of these turrets in April 1989, which resulted
in 47 deaths; the damage has never been repaired.

  Tomahawk cruise-missiles are in eight, four-cell, elevating armoured boxes
and these missiles were used with great success against targets deep in Iraq
during the Gulf War. The Harpoons are placed in fixed, four-missile canisters
abreast the after stack.

  In the defence rundown following the end of the Cold War it was decided to
mothball USS *Iowa* and USS *New Jersey* in FY 1991, but USS *Wisconsin* and
USS *Missouri* were both still on active duty when the Gulf War broke out and
deployed to the Middle East. Both these ships may now be paid-off yet again,
but there is no current intention to scrap any of the four, despite their age. So,
like sleeping giants, they will await the next call to return to active duty.

**Right: Nearing her 50th birthday, USS *Wisconsin* (BB 64) remains a
truly awesome sight, and can still pack a mighty "punch".**

**Overleaf: An example of that "punch" being thrown, as all nine of her
massive 16in (406mm) guns let rip at a distant land target.**

Landing Craft, Air-Cushion

Hovercraft
85 in class.

Country of origin: United States.
Displacement: 87.2 tons light (170-202 tons full load).
Dimensions: Length overall 88ft (26.8m); beam 47ft (14.3m); draught (off cushion) 2.9ft (0.9m).
Armament: Two 0.5in (12.7mm) machine-guns.
Propulsion: Four Avco-Lycoming gas-turbines (1,5820bhp); two shrouded reversible-pitch propellers for thrust; 40kts.

One major development in amphibious warfare is the air-cushion craft, which started off as a small prototype over 25 years ago and is now a large and sophisticated military vehicle. However, all of these craft are confined to a coastal role and attempts to create a true ocean-going version are still very much plans for the future.

Trials in the United States have now led to a viable 150-ton craft capable of over 40kts. There are side walls enclosing the cargo and housing the pilots' position and the engines. The centre area is devoted to cargo which comprises 25 troops and one main battle tank or an equivalent load of up to 70 tons. The bow ramp measures nearly 30ft (9.09m) whilst the stern ramps is half that size.

Unfortunately, noise and dust levels are high and spay suppressors are fitted along the skirts to improve the pilots' view. Heavy seas also pose a serious problem during operations.

The original plan called for 96 craft but the programme is likely to end at 85. These unique craft have no equal in the conventional types of landing craft that can only cross some 15 per cent of the world's coastline, whereas the LCAC can cross 70 per cent.

Above: A trio of US Navy LCACs ride the waves and head for a beach landing. Note the large, reversible-pitch propellers.

Below: This high-angle view clearly reveals the ample cargo space, used for both men and machinery. Spray suppressors have been incorporated in the skirt to enhance pilot vision.

Los Angeles (SSN 688) Class

Nuclear-powered attack submarines
47 boats (SSN 688-SSN 725, SSN 750-SSN 758); 15 building (SSN 759-SSN 773).

Country of origin: United States.
Displacement: 6,927 tons.
Dimensions: Length 360.0ft (109.7m); beam 33.1ft (10.1m); draught 32.1ft (9,8m).
Armament: Four 21in (533mm) tubes for torpedoes, Tomahawk SLCM, Harpoon SSM, etc (22 reloads); **SSN 719 et seq:** 12 Mk 36 vertical tubes for Tomahawk; **SSN 756 et seq:** mines.
Propulsion: Two GE S6G pressurized water-cooled nuclear reactors; two geared turbines; 35,000shp; one shaft; 30 + kts.

The origins of the Los Angeles (SSN 688) class go back to the late-1960s when the US Navy considered a requirement for a high-speed attack and ASW submarine. The result of that study has been one of the most sophisticated and expensive, but very effective and important weapons systems ever to have attained operational status, and one which will eventually number no less than 62 boats. The Los Angeles class submarines are 67.9ft (20.7m) longer than the previous Sturgeon class and the hull is optimized for high submerged speed, with a very small sail. The first-of-class USS *Los Angeles* (SSN 688) was commissioned on 13 November 1976, since when building has continued at a steady rate; the 62nd and last-of-class will be commissioned in 1997.

As initially built, the forward hydroplanes are mounted on the sail, limiting the ability of those boats so fitted to penetrate the ice in Arctic waters. However, from USS *San Juan* (SSN 751) onwards, the planes have been moved forward to the more traditional bow position and, together with some new electronic equipment, this enables them to be formally declared "Arctic capable".

The most remarkable feature of the Los Angeles class is its armament. These powerful submarines are armed with Sub-Harpoon and Tomahawk missiles,

Above: USS *Miami* (SSN 755) takes to the water on 30 June 1990. She is the 44th example of her class, out of 62 planned.

as well as conventional and wire-guided torpedoes. From USS *Providence* (SSN 719) onwards they are also equipped with 12 vertical launch tubes, which enable Tomahawk to be carried without reducing the quantity of other weapons carried internally.

During their service these submarines have carried out many remarkable feats, one of them being the circumnavigation of the globe, totally submerged, by USS *Groton* (SSN 694), between 4 April and 8 October 1980. Several of them also fired Tomahawk missiles whilst submerged against targets deep in Iraq during the Gulf War of 1991.

Below: With her pennant number clearly visible on the sail, USS *Oklahoma City* (SSN 723) proudly shows the "stars 'n' stripes".

Nimitz Class

Nuclear-powered aircraft carriers
Five ships (CVN 68-CVN 72); three building (CVN 73-CVN 75).

Country of origin: United States.
Displacement: 93,900 tons full load.
Dimensions: Length 1,091.9ft (332.8m); beam — hull 134.2ft (40.9m); flight-deck 253.0ft (77.1m); draught 37.1ft (11.3m).
Aircraft: 24 Grumman F-14A Tomcat, 24 McDonnell Douglas F/A-18 Hornet, 10 Grumman A-6E Intruder, four Grumman KA-6D Intruder, four Grumman EA-6B Prowler, four Grumman E-2C Hawkeye, 10 Lockheed S-3A/B Viking, six Sikorsky SH-3H Sea King or Sikorsky SH-60B Seahawk.
Armament: Three Mk 29 launchers for Sea Sparrow SAM; three 0.8in (20mm) Mk 15 CIWS (CVN 70 has 4).
Propulsion: Two pressurized water A4W/A1G nuclear reactors; (280,000shp); four shafts; 30+kts.

The replacement of the Midway class of aircraft carriers started to be discussed in the mid-1960s and there was no doubt in the Department of the Navy that the success of the USS *Enterprise* (CVN 65) demonstrated conclusively that nuclear propulsion provided the best answer — although the capital costs of construction were enormous, even by American standards. Indeed, it was because of the awesome costs of constructing nuclear carriers that Congress had insisted in October 1963 that USS *John F. Kennedy* (CV 67) should be powered by fuel-oil rather than nuclear reactors. However, there had been many advances since the construction of CVN 65, not least being that the eight A2W reactors used in the earlier ship could be replaced by just two A4W reactors, giving the same power. Furthermore, the uranium cores would need to be replaced less often than on the earlier ship.

After much discussion funds were provided for USS *Nimitz* (CVN 68) on 1 July 1966, with completion scheduled for 1971, and her sisters (CVN 69 and CVN 70), due in 1973 and 1975 respectively. Unfortunately, the programme was subjected to repeated delays, but eventually the problems were overcome and the ships joined the fleet at regular intervals: USS *Nimitz* (CVN 68), 3 May 1975; USS *Dwight D. Eisenhower* (CVN 69), 18 October 1977; USS *Carl Vinson* (CVN 70), 13 March 1982; USS *Theodore Roosevelt* (CVN 71), 25 October 1986; and USS

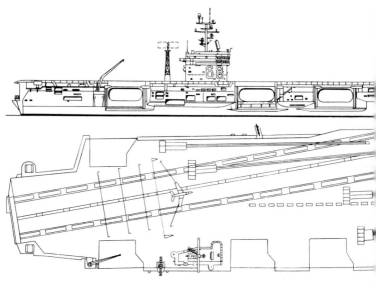

Above: The perfect example of force projection in action, as the second-of-class, USS *Dwight D. Eisenhower* (CVN 69) steams through the Suez Canal in September 1990, as part of the build-up to Operation *Desert Storm*. Worthy of note in this head-on view is the angled flight-deck, complete with a pair of catapults for dual-launch operations.

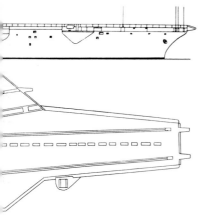

Left: The mighty ships that constitute the Nimitz class displace just under 94,000 tons when fully loaded, and can accommodate well over 80 combat aircraft at anyone time. Their war complement, including all of the onboard aviation staff, is an incredible 6,286 men.

Abraham Lincoln (CVN 72), 11 November 1989. The remaining three will be commissioned at two year intervals: USS *George Washington* (CVN 73) in 1993; USS *John C. Stennis* (CVN 74) in 1995; and USS *United States* (CVN 75) in 1997.

It will be noted from this list that the programme has expanded from the original three carriers. USS *Theodore Roosevelt* (CVN 71) was ordered in FY 1980 after another long-running battle between the Pentagon and the Carter Administration, the latter wanting either a cheaper 62,000-ton design or a repeat of the USS *John F. Kennedy* (CV 67) design. The next two carriers were ordered in FY 1983 and the final pair in June 1988. These five ships have slight differences from the first three, which sometimes leads to them being referred to as a separate, Roosevelt class. All eight carriers are being constructed at the Newport News Yard, the only one in the United States now capable of building nuclear-propelled warships of this size.

The dimensions and layout of the flight-deck on the Nimitz class are virtually identical with those on USS *John F. Kennedy*, the last of the Kitty Hawk class. However, in comparison with USS *Enterprise*, the reduction in the number of reactors permitted major improvements in the internal arrangements below hangar-deck level. The propulsion machinery is divided between two rooms with some of the magazines in the space between them, and there is a 20 per cent increase in the volume of aviation fuel (sufficient for 16 days of flying at a steady rate), munitions and stores that can be carried. The nuclear cores will provide power for these splendid carriers for 13 years of operation in the first three ships and for an astonishing 15 years in the remainder. The combat power concentrated in these hulls is enormous, but this requires a large amount of equipment and manpower, too. There are 86 aircraft and 6,286 men — a major concentration of resources and a very attractive target in a major conflict! Also, the ships are extremely expensive: for example, the two ships ordered in FY83 cost $6,559 million (at 1983 prices), which does not include the cost of the Air Wing! USS *Nimitz* is scheduled to last until at least 2020, the other carriers making up the class even longer.

Right: No less than 61 aircraft can be seen on the flight-deck of USS *Carl Vinson* (CVN 70) in this revealing portrait — and a further 20 or so aircraft are below deck! Nearest the camera, on the stern, sit Grumman F-14A Tomcat fleet defence fighters.

Below: Another view of USS *Carl Vinson* (CVN 70), the third of the Nimitz class aircraft carriers to be built. As with all her sisterships in the Nimitz class (those now in service and those planned for service in the future), she was built by the Virginia-based Newport News Shipbuilding and Dry Dock Company Inc.

Ohio Class

Nuclear-powered ballistic missile submarines
12 boats (SSBN 726-SSBN 737); five building (SSBN 738-SSBN 742); one projected (SSBN 743).

Country of origin: United States.
Displacement: 18,750 tons.
Dimensions: Length 560.0ft (170.7m); beam 42.0ft (12.18); draught 36.4ft (11.8m).
Armament: SSBN 726 — SSBN 733: 24 Trident I (C-4) SLBM; **SSBN 734 onwards:** Trident II (D-5) SLBM; **all boats:** four 21in (533mm) tubes for Gould Mk 48 torpedoes.
Propulsion: One GE S8G natural circulation pressurized water-cooled nuclear reactor turbo-reduction drive; 60,000shp; one shaft; 20 + kts.

Development of the Trident I SLBM started in the early-1970s and it quickly became clear that a new type of SSBN would be needed to take advantage of these new missiles. At first these were to have been enlarged versions of the Lafayette class, using the same Westinghouse S5W nuclear reactor. However, the need to reduce noise levels led to the adoption of the natural-circulation nuclear reactor then being tested, while it was considered most cost-effective to design the submarine to take 24 rather than 18 missiles. Congress baulked at the enormous costs, but this changed to support when the Soviet Navy introduced the 3,650nm (6,935km) range SS-N-8 SLBM in the Delta class SSBN (q.v.).

The programme has suffered from many problems and delays, but the eventual outcome is an excellent submarine and an extremely potent missile. The first-of-class, USS *Ohio* (SSBN 736), ran trials from June 1981, making her first

Below: A close-up view of the USS *Pennsylvania* (SSBN 735) at sea. These "boomers" can stay at sea for up to 70 days at a time.

Above: Positioning of the sail well forward allows a long and clear deck abaft, under which sit 24 Trident I/II SLBMs.

operational deployment in October 1982 and firing her first operational missile in January 1982. The first eight Ohio class boats are armed with 24 Trident I (C-5) missiles, mounted vertically abaft the sail. The newer Trident II (D-5) missile is fitted to USS *Tennessee* (SSBN 734) and subsequent submarines, and the former boat started her first operational cruise with this weapon in March 1990. Trident II (D-5) will later be retrofitted to the first eight of the class. All these submarines have four conventional torpedo tubes, but would only expect to use such weapons for self-defence and as a last resort.

The great increase in range of the Trident missile means that they can be based in the USA, with the first eight Ohios operating out of Bangor, Maine, and the remainder out of King's Bay, Georgia. This also means that the majority of their patrols will be conducted in US-dominated waters.

The normal operating schedule is a 70-day patrol with one crew, followed by a 25-day refit and then another patrol with a different crew; major refits, lasting one year each, are needed only once every nine years, which coincide with the lift expectancy of the nuclear core. This gives each submarine an operational availability of 66 per cent — an exceptional figure.

The Soviet Typhoon class submarines (pages 98-101) are larger than the Ohio class, but carry four less missiles and have, in any case, proved far less successful in service. With the end of the Cold War in the late-1980s, followed by the collapse of Soviet power in 1991, it is highly unlikely that production of the Ohio class will continue beyond the currently programmed 18 boats.

Oliver Hazard Perry (FFG 7) Class

Guided-missile frigates
USA — 51 (FFG 7-FFG 16, FFG 19-FFG 34, FFG 36-FFG 43, FFG 45-FFG 61); **Australia** — five (01-05), one building (06); **Spain** — four (F 81-F 84), two building (F 85-F 86); **Taiwan** — 12 building.

Country of origin: United States.
Displacement: 3,658 tons (short hull), 4,100 tons (long hull).
Dimensions: Length overall (short hull) 444.9ft (135.6m), (long hull) 455.4ft (138.8m); beam 44.9ft (13.7m); draught 19ft (5.8m).
Aircraft: One Kaman SH-2F Seasprite LAMPS I helicopter (short hull), one/two Sikorsky SH-60B Seahawk LAMPS III helicopter (long hull).
Armament: One Mk 13 Mod 4 launcher for Harpoon SSM and Standard SM-1 MR SAM; one 3in (76mm) Mk 75 DP gun, one 0.8in (20mm) Mk 15 gatling CIWS; six 12.7in (324mm) ASW torpedo tubes.
Propulsion: Two GE LM-2500 gas-turbines; one shaft; 29kts.

The Oliver Hazard Perry (FFG 7) class was designed in the early-1970s as the cheaper component of a high/low technology mix and was intended to provide a large number of escorts with reduced capabilities and thus reduced price. These were intended to balance the very expensive, specialized ASW and AAW ships needed to protect carriers, and strict limits were placed on cost, displacement and manpower.

These ships have been built in smaller yards, utilizing simpler construction techniques, making maximum use of flat panels and bulkheads, and keeping internal passageways as straight as possible. Propulsion is by two gas-turbines, but, as with earlier US frigates there is only one propeller. One unusual feature is that two small, retractable "propulsion pods" are fitted to provide emergency "get-you-home" power and to assist in docking; each pod has a 325hp engine and both can propel the ship at about 6kts.

The single Mk 13 launcher arm on the foredeck can launch either Standard SAMs (36 carried) or Harpoon SSMs (4 carried). A 3in (76mm) Mk 75 gun turret

Below: An example of strength in depth, with a trio of Oliver Hazard Perry class frigates on patrol. In the foreground is USS *Jack Williams* (FFG 24), flanked by USS *Antrim* (FFG 20) and the first-of-class, USS *Oliver Hazard Perry* (FFG 7).

licence-built OTO Melara Compact) is atop the superstructure just forward of a very abbreviated stack. A 0.8in (20mm) Mk 15 CIWS is mounted on the roof of the hangar. ASROC is not carried and the only ASW weapons on the ship are two triple 12.7in (324mm) torpedo tubes.

The flight-deck and hangar can handle a Kaman SH-2F Seasprite LAMPS I helicopter, but not the newer and more effective Sikorsky SH-60B Seahawk LAMPS III. This problem was solved in a neat and economic manner by angling out the transom to 45deg, which extends the overall length of the ship by 10.4ft (3.16m) without altering the waterline length, and enables a Recovery Assistance, Securing and Traversing system (RAST) to be fitted. Other modifications were also made, including fitting fin stablizers. This new layout was trialled aboard USS *McInerny* (FFG 8) and then incorporated as standard during construction into USS *Underwood* (FFG 36) and subsequent ships. It is also being fitted into some of the earlier ships during refits.

These ships have proved to be very capable in service and are actually used more as general-purpose destroyers than as "escorts". As a result they have had much extra equipment put in and, despite a design full load displacement of 3,600 tons with a 39 tons growth margin, they now displace some 4,100 tons at full load! Many have served in the Gulf, where USS *Stark* (FFG 31) was hit by two Exocets (one of which did not explode) and another, USS *Samuel B. Roberts* (FFG 58) hit a mine; both survived, returned to the USA for repairs and are now back in service.

The design has proved popular abroad. Four were built in the USA for the Royal Australian Navy with a further two now under construction in Australia itself. Another six are being built by Bazan for the Spanish Navy (Santa Maria class), with a probability of another six to replace the cancelled NATO NFR90 project. Finally, Taiwan is building six to the standard design (PFG-2-I class) and six to a modified design (PFG-2-II class) incoporating a 17ft (5.18m) plug and considerably modified armament.

Right: The foredeck of the Oliver Hazard Perry class frigate design is dominated by the single Mk 13 Mod 4 SAM/SSM launcher unit.

Below: The unusual profile of the superstructure is shown to good effect in this view of USS *Oliver Hazard Perry* (FFG 7).

Spruance Class

Destroyers
31 ships (DD 963-DD 992, DD 997).

Country of origin: United States.
Displacement: 8,040 tons.
Dimensions: Length overall 563.3ft (171.7m); beam 55.1ft (16.8m); draught 19.0ft (5.8m).
Aircraft: One Kaman SH-2F Seasprite LAMPS I or one Sikorsky SH-60B Seahawk LAMPS III ASW helicopter.
Armament: Seven ships (**DDs 974, 976, 979, 983-984, 989-990**): two Mk 44 quad box launchers for eight BGM-109 Tomahawk SLCM; two quad launchers for eight RGM-84A Harpoon SSM; six Mk 32 12.7in (324mm) tubes for 14 Mk 46 torpedoes (to be replaced by Mk 50 torpedoes); one Mk 29 octuple launcher for 24 Sea Sparrow SAM; 24 Mk 16 octuple launchers for ASROC; two Mk 45 Mod 0/1 5in (127mm) guns, two Mk 15 Vulcan Phalanx 0.8in (20mm) CIWS; four 0.5in (12.7mm) machine-guns. **All others:** as above except Mk 44 launchers replaced by one Mk 41 Mod 0 61-missile VLS for 45 BGM-109 Tomahawk SLCM and ASROC; Mk 16 octuple launchers for ASROC deleted.
Propulsion: Four GE LM-2500 gas-turbines (86,000shp); two shafts; 32.5kts.

By the 1960s the large number of Second World War-vintage destroyers serving in the US Navy were worn-out and in urgent need of replacement, and the Spruance class was designed to replace them. They are much larger ships, intended principally for ASW work. One of the aims was to build as many ships as possible with the money available; so, although they are large and very seaworthy ships, they have a relatively small number of weapons systems for their hull-size. One of the measures intended to keep costs down was the use of a Total Procurement Package, which involved placing the entire production responsibility with one company at one site, which led to muddle, causing delays and

Below: Large and roomy, but relatively lightly-armed for their size, the Spruances are undergoing a major updating programme.

Above: A Tactical Display System suite undergoes a "shakedown" inside one Spruance class ship's Combat Information Centre. The class excels in the realm of anti-submarine warfare operations.

cost-overruns. Thirty ships were ordered, but the US Congress later added to the confusuion by insisting on an order for a 31st to an "air-capable" design, with an enlarged hangar for four helicopters. The ship, USS *Hayler* (DD 997), was completed, but as a virtually standard Spruance class design.

The success of the basic design is shown by the fact that both the Kidd class destroyers and the Ticonderoga class cruisers use virtually the same hull, which was designed to provide minimum rolling and pitching without the use of stabilizers. All three classes also use the same propulsion system, which is provided by four General Electric LM-2500 gas-turbines, which, at the time of its appearance, was the first such installation in a major US warship. It is controlled by just one operator at a central station and has proved both efficient and very quiet in service, being able to accelerate the ship from 12 to 32kts in just 53 seconds. The gas-turbines are paired, with two coupled through reduction gearing to each shaft, and cruising range can be greatly extended by closing-down one engine on each shaft.

Naturally, the armament and sensors installed in these ships have undergone change and development since they entered service, one indication being that the crew has increased from 232 enlisted men to the present 315, an increase of 36 per cent! In addition, individual ships have often been used for "one-off" tests of new systems. As a result, at any one time there are marked variations in the weapons across the class.

In 1974 the then Shah of Iran placed an order for six developments of the Spruance class, which were to be the core of his rapidly expanding navy. The order was later reduced to four, but after Ayatollah Khomeini took over the order was cancelled. Fortunately, Congress authorized completion of these ships for the US Navy and they joined the fleet in 1981/82 as the Kidd (DDG 993) class at the "bargain" price of $510 million each. They use the Spruance hull, but are optimized for the air defence role, with two Mk 29 launchers for Standard SM-1 MR SAMs and an SPS-48E 3-D radar. They are very well fitted-out and as their air-conditioning was designed for service with the Iranian Navy have proved very effective for Gulf deployments under the US flag!

Below: Commissioned in May 1978, USS *John Young* is the 11th Sprunance class destroyer. A further 20 have been commissioned.

Tarawa Class

Amphibious assault ships
Five ships: LHA 1-LHA 5.

Country of origin: United States.
Displacement: 8,040 tons.
Dimensions: Length overall 834ft (254.2m); beam 131ft 9in (40.2m); draught 25ft 9in (7.9m).
Aircraft: Typically, 16 Boeing-Vertol CH-46 Sea Knight, six Sikorsky CH-53 Sea Stallion, four Bell UH-1N Iroquois helicopters.
Armament: Two 5in (127mm) Mk 45 DP guns, two 0.8in (20mm) Mk 15 gatling CIWS; six 0.8in (20mm) Mk 67 AA guns.
Propulsion: Two sets Westinghouse geared turbines (77,000shp); two shafts; 24kts.

The Tarawa class Amphibious Assault Ships (LHAs) are designed to fulfil the functions of both the LPHs and the LPDs, by being able to carry a battalion group of about 1,800 Marines and land them and their equipment by both helicopters and landing craft. Although this means that the loss of one ship would be more damaging than before, it saves the cost of a large and complex vessel and its crew. They have a full length continuous flight deck, with a large rectangular island to starboard. The helicopter hangar is in the aft part of the ship, and it is connected to the flight deck by a portside elevator and another at the stern on the centerline. The forward part of the hull at hangar deck level is used for stores and equipment, which, as in the Iwo Jimas, is brought up to the flight deck by two small elevators. Beneath the hangar aft there is a dock large enough to contain four 1610 class LCUs.

Above: Four landing craft can be carried by the Tarawa class LCAs.

Side thrusters are fitted to make docking and undocking easier. Nine of these ships were ordered under a Total Package Procurement Contract from Litton Industries, but as with the case of the Spruances this has proved a failure. Completion of the class was delayed but the fifth and last ship, USS *Peleliu* (LHA 5), was commissioned in May 1980. The Wasp class is now under construction, this being a modified version of USS *Tarawa* (LHA 1) capable of being used as either an assault transport or as an ASW carrier.

Below: In addition to the landing craft carried in the dock, each Tarawa class LCA is able to carry some 1,800 fully-equipped Marines, up to 45 tractors, and 1,200 tons of aviation fuel.

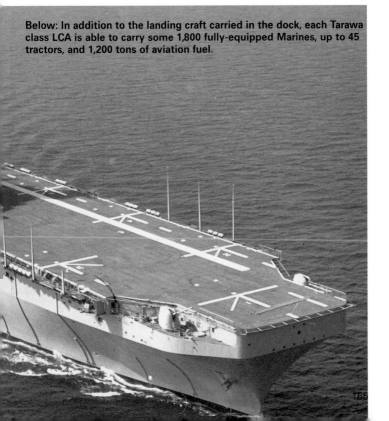

Ticonderoga Class

Guided missile cruisers
20 ships (CG 47-CG 66); seven building (CG 67-CG 73).

Country of origin: United States.
Displacement: 7,015 tons standard (9,407-9,590 tons full load)
Dimensions: Length overall 567ft (172.8m); beam 55ft (16.8m); draught 31ft sonar (9.5m).
Armament: Four ships (**CG 47-CG 50**): two quad launchers for eight RGM-84A Harpoon SSM; two twin Mk 26 Mod 5 launchers for 68 Standard SM-2MR SAM and 20 ASROC; six 12.7in (324mm) tubes for Mk 46 Mod 5 torpedoes (to be replaced by Mk 50 torpedoes); two Mk 45 Mod 0.5in (127mm) machine-guns. **CG 51**: as above but Mk 45 Mod 0 guns replaced by two Mk 45 Mod 1 5in (127mm) guns. **CG 52 onwards**: as above but Mk 26 Mod 5 launchers replaced by two Mk41 Mod 0 VLS for 28 BGM-109 Tomahawk SLCM, 122 Standard SM-2MR SAM and 20 ASROC; two Mk 45 Mod 1 5in (127mm) DP guns.
Aircraft: Two Kaman SH-2F Seasprite LAMPS I or two Sikorsky SH-60B Seahawk LAMPS III helicopters.
Propulsion: Four General Electric gas-turbines (80,000hp); two shafts; 30kts.

This large group of warships, specially developed to provide adequate defence for a Carrier Battle Group against air attack and anti-ship missiles, form the most effective anti-air warfare system currently deployed by the US Navy. They also sport a full and comprehensive anti-submarine warfare capability. But such a force does not come cheap: each vessel costs some $1,065 million.

Above: USS *Bunker Hill* (CG 52) leads the guided-missile cruiser USS *Long Beach* (CGN 9) during operations in Gulf waters.

Below: One of 68 Standard SM-2MR SAMs aboard USS *Ticonderoga* (CG 47) streaks skywards to intercept an incoming air "threat".

The first-of-class, USS *Ticonderoga* (CG 47), was laid down in January 1980 and commissioned three years later. To date, 27 vessels have been authorized, their role being to act as air and missile defence systems for the US Navy's 13 Carrier Battle Groups. The original plan called for the construction of a group of nuclear-powered escorts similar to the modified Virginia class, but the enormous cost of the nuclear propulsion and the newly-emerging AEGIS system rendered this plan unfeasible.

The AEGIS system is one of the major breakthroughs in naval technology, and was developed as a counter to the likely saturation by Soviet missiles of Carrier Battle Groups. The system can cope with this form of attack simply because it is able to react instantaneously and has unlimited tracking ability; unlike existing radar systems that can track and process only a limited number of targets.

The Ticonderoga class vessels are based on the Spruance class design, using the same basic hull and a lengthened version of the gas turbine propulsion system. Thus, great savings were achieved in the programme costs. The superstructure has been enlarged to carry the AEGIS/SPY-1 system, with two large fixed-array radar antennae on the forward superstructure (one facing forward, the other to starboard), and a second group positioned on the sides of the after deck house (one facing aft, the other to port). Each comprises a total of 4,100 radiating elements and is controlled by a UYK-1 computer, which classifies and prioritizes each tracked target.

The complete AEGIS system was used to good effect off the coast of Libya during the mid- to late-1980s, leading to a significant reduction in the number of combat air patrols by Libyan fighters over US Navy task force vessels. The system also aided the air- and carrier-launched attacks by US forces on Libyan targets as part of Operation *El Dorado Canyon*.

The system's great advantage is its extended tracking range, thus providing defences with more time in which to prepare and react, and the ability to send

data to other vessels instantaneously. However, when operating close to shore, its early warning ability is somewhat reduced.

During construction of USS *Ticonderoga*, a series of design changes were introduced to improve the type's sea-keeping qualities. Bow bulwarks were added to reduce the amount of water taken on board because of the greater draught compared to that of the original Spruance design. Higher exhaust stacks were also added. From USS *Vincennes* (CG 49) onwards, a lattice tripod mast has been added amidships in order to save approximately nine tons in weight.

A highly impressive array of armament includes a combination of land attack and anti-ship BGM-109 Tomahawk SLCM, these being fitted as standard from USS *Bunker Hill* (CG 52) onwards. Eight such missiles are carried in each Vertical Launch System (VLS), with a further 12 rounds held in reserve in the magazine. Evaluation of the VLS continues, and vertically-launched ASROC will be retrofitted as and when available.

Long-range airborne targets are dealt with courtesy of the Standard SM-2MR SAM, up to 18 of which can be controlled in the air at any one time, with another four primed and ready for firing. Close-range defence is the domain of the two Vulcan Phalanx Mk 15 CIWS, each of which can be fired at a rate of 3,000 rounds-per-minute. The two 5in (127mm) Mk 45 guns are suitable only for anti-surface target work, and have a rate-of-fire of 20 rounds-per-minute.

All Ticonderoga class vessels will eventually incorporate a series of modifications to their missile systems and onboard computers as part of a Long Range Improvement Programme (Baselines 0 to IV). A further 10 such advanced vessels are required by the US Navy, but funding has yet to be approved to permit their construction.

Below: USS *Vincennes* (CG 49) demonstrated its firepower when it brought down an Iran Air A300 airliner with SAMs in 1988.